READER'S DIGEST
The Creative Kitchen
POULTRY

The Reader's Digest Association (Canada) Ltd. • Montreal • Pleasantville, New York

Editor	Patricia Sylvester
Designer	Andrée Payette
Copy Editor	Francis Legge
Coordination	Susan Wong
Production	Holger Lorenzen
Art Direction	John McGuffie
Index	Natalie King
Cover Photograph	Le Groupe Becdor

The acknowledgments that appear on page 148 are hereby made a part of this copyright page.

Copyright ©1985 The Reader's Digest Association (Canada) Ltd.
Copyright ©1985 The Reader's Digest Association, Inc.
Copyright ©1985 Reader's Digest Association Far East Ltd.
Philippine Copyright 1985 Reader's Digest Association Far East Ltd.

Reproduction in any manner, in whole or in part, in English or in other languages, is prohibited. All rights reserved.

FIRST EDITION

ISBN 0-88850-134-X

85 86 87 88 / 5 4 3 2 1

Printed in Canada

Table of Contents

Poultry Basics	4
Poultry Stuffings	8
Poultry Stock, Gravy, and Sauces	10
Recipes	
Chicken	12
Chicken Livers	100
Cornish Hen	103
Duck	104
Goose	116
Guinea Hen	118
Turkey	122
Ingredient Substitutions	141
Recipes by Name and Time	142
Index	145
Acknowledgments	148

Symbols

⌛ Less than 1 hour preparing and cooking time

⌛ ⌛ 1–2 hours preparing and cooking time

⌛ ⌛ ⌛ More than 2 hours preparing and cooking time

 Cooking tip

 Supplementary recipe

Sizes of Chickens

Very small   Less than 3 pounds
      Small   3–5 pounds
  Medium   5–6 pounds
      Large   More than 6 pounds

Poultry Basics

Most poultry is sold ready for cooking—that is, hung, plucked, and drawn. Oven-ready frozen poultry must be thawed slowly before cooking. It should be left in its wrapping and placed in a refrigerator for 24–48 hours, depending on size, to thaw. It should never be immersed in hot or warm water, although small parts may be held under cold running water to hasten thawing.

Chicken. This meat is tender, mild flavored, easily digested, and lean. Much of its fat content is unsaturated—and a good portion of the fat is in the skin, which dieters can easily discard.

Broilers (also called fryers) are young birds weighing up to 4 pounds. They are very tender and can be fried, baked, broiled, roasted, or barbecued.

Roasters are a bit older than broilers and weigh over 4 pounds. Their larger size makes them ideal for roasting, but they can also be barbecued or fried.

Stewing hens (also called fowl or stewing chicken) are mature, less tender birds weighing 3 pounds or more. An economical buy, they are best braised or stewed.

Capons are young, desexed males, bred to give a high proportion of white meat. Generally weighing from 5–8 pounds, capons are larger than most chickens. Exceptionally tender, they are best roasted. Due to the cost of neutering, however, capon production is declining.

Guinea hens, or guinea fowl, were originally game birds. The flesh is firm and creamy-white with a slightly pheasant-like flavor. Weighing as much as 4 pounds, they are particularly suitable for braising.

Rock Cornish hens are the smallest type of chicken, weighing about 1 pound. They have a plump, meaty breast, are very tender, and provide 1 serving apiece.

Turkey. Usually sold as whole, frozen birds, turkey is also available fresh or in parts.

Self-basting or prebasted turkeys have been injected with water and fat, and don't need extra basting.

POULTRY STORAGE LIMITS		
Poultry	Maximum refrigerator storage 40°F	Maximum freezer storage 0°F
Chicken, turkey whole parts	2–3 days 2–3 days	1 year 6 months
Duck, goose	2–3 days	3 months

CUTTING UP POULTRY

1. Pull leg away from the body and slice through flesh to joint, using a very sharp knife.

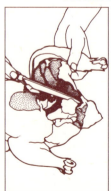

2. Break off legs using a knife to sever tendons. The leg can be divided into drumstick and thigh.

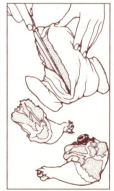

3. Cut through flesh and joint to remove wing, being careful not to slice off breast meat.

4. Separate the breast from the lower carcass.

5. Cut breast in half crosswise, or bend it lengthwise along breastbone, until it snaps.

TRUSSING POULTRY WITH A NEEDLE

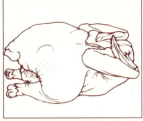
1. *Fold wings over neck.*

2. *Slit skin above tail.*

3. *Slip tail into slit.*

4. *Push needle through body.*

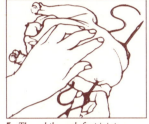
5. *Thread through first joint.*

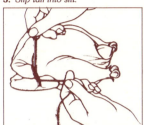
6. *Secure string at wings.*

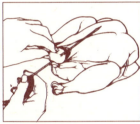
7. *Thread through tail.*

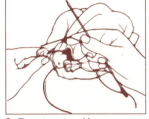
8. *Tie string around legs.*

9. *Secure string tightly at legs.*

Broilers are young birds weighing up to 10 pounds. Tender, they're ideal for broiling, roasting, and barbecuing.

Young turkeys are larger than broilers and are best suited for roasting.

Mature turkeys are more than 8 months of age and are not as tender as younger ones. They are best braised or stewed, or added to soups or salads.

Turkey wings are meaty and make tasty substitutes for fried chicken.

POULTRY YIELDS	
1 pound cooked boneless meat	3¼ cups diced meat
1 pound raw boneless meat	2 cups cooked diced meat
1 pound raw turkey breast, bone in	13 ounces raw boneless turkey 9 ounces cooked boneless turkey
1 pound raw chicken breast, bone in	9 ounces raw boneless chicken 7 ounces cooked boneless chicken

Duck. This meat is dark with a higher percentage of fat and bone than chicken or turkey. Most ducks are frozen whole young ducks (also called ducklings) less than 1 year old. Weighing around 4–6 pounds, young duck is good for roasting.

Goose. A fatty bird with dark, game-flavored flesh, goose is less tender than duck, chicken, or turkey. Most goose sold is frozen young goose, weighing from 9–12 pounds. Young goose, 1 year old or less, is the most tender, but a bird weighing less than 8 pounds has little meat on its bones.

Boning Poultry
Breast meat is boned one side at a time. Starting at the large end of the breast, cut away meat from the breastbone and rib cage, pulling as you cut.

Skinning Poultry
Pull skin gently off the poultry, using a knife to sever connective tissue.

Cooking Methods

Roasting is the most popular method of cooking whole chicken, capon, duck, goose, guinea hen, and turkey. With the exception of duck and goose, which are fatty birds, all poultry should be barded (covered with thin slices of pork fat or strips of bacon) or generously brushed with butter or oil before and during roasting.

Poaching and steaming are suitable methods for cooking older birds and poultry parts. The cooked flesh is mainly used in other dishes, such as fricassees. Braising and casseroling are ideal, though slow ways to cook older birds or poultry parts.

Roasting

Stuffing. A stuffing improves the flavor and appearance of poultry, and it also makes the meat go further.

Stuffings are based on bread crumbs made from day-old bread, meat, and rice to which melted butter is added, together with herbs and seasonings. Because a stuffing expands during cooking, it is necessary to stuff the bird loosely; a basic 2-cup stuffing or forcemeat mixture is enough for a 3½-pound chicken.

Trussing. Once stuffed, the bird should be trussed so that it will keep its shape during cooking. Trussed poultry also looks more attractive when it reaches the table. To tie up a bird, use a trussing needle that has an eye large enough to take a piece of fine string (see illustrations on page 5). If a trussing needle is not available, use poultry skewers and string to secure the bird.

Barding. After trussing, the bird is ready for cooking. If it is to be roasted, the lean breast flesh should be protected to prevent it from drying out. This is known as barding and consists of covering the breast with pork fat or bacon. Barding is not necessary for duck or goose. However, chicken and turkey have drier flesh and benefit from barding.

Bacon is preferable to pork fat because it adds flavor to the poultry. During cooking, the fat from the bacon melts and bastes the flesh, thus keeping it moist. About 20 minutes before the end of cooking time, remove the crisp bacon slices from the breast and return the bird to the oven so that the breast will brown.

ROASTING TIMES FOR TURKEY		
Weight	325°F	450°F
6–8 pounds	3 –3½ hours	2¼ –2½ hours
8–10 pounds	3½ –3¾ hours	2½ –2¾ hours
10–14 pounds	3¾ –4¼ hours	2¾ –3 hours
14–18 pounds	4¼ –4¾ hours	3 –3½ hours
18–20 pounds	4¾ –5¼ hours	3½ –3¾ hours
20–24 pounds	5¼ –6 hours	3¾ –4¼ hours

Roasting. A roasting chicken weighing 3½–4 pounds will serve 3–4 persons. Place the barded or well-buttered chicken on a rack on its side in a roasting pan in the center of an oven preheated to 375°F. Allow 20 minutes on each side plus 20 minutes on its back for a chicken weighing 3½–4 pounds. Baste well.

A chicken weighing 4–6 pounds will give 4–6 servings. It should be roasted at 325°F, allowing 25 minutes on each side plus 25 minutes on the back.

A capon with an average weight of 6–8 pounds provides 8–10 portions; it should be roasted on a rack at 325°F.

Alternatively, loosely wrap the chicken in foil and roast at 400°–425°F, allowing 20 minutes per pound plus an extra 20 minutes. Open the foil 20 minutes before cooking is complete to allow the bird to brown. Use a skewer to test the bird for doneness. Insert the skewer through the thickest part of the thigh; if clear juices run out, the bird is cooked.

Allow ¾ pound oven-ready weight of turkey per person. Include stuffing in this calculation. Turkey should be particularly well barded, unless it is prebasted.

Roasting methods for turkey depend on the size of the bird and the time available. At low oven temperature (325°F), the turkey must be frequently basted with its own juices, even if it is barded. At a higher temperature (450°F), which saves at least an hour of cooking time, wrap the bird loosely in aluminum foil to prevent the flesh from drying out. About ½ hour before cooking is complete, open the foil to allow the skin of the bird to become brown and crisp.

Duck is prepared for roasting in the same way as chicken. As a rule, it is inadvisable to stuff duck with bread stuffing; the crumbs may absorb too much fat and become indigestible. Because duck is a fatty bird, it does not need barding or brushing with butter before cooking, but the skin should be pricked all over with a needle to allow the fat to run out of the bird during cooking. Season the duck with salt and freshly ground pepper and cook in a moderately hot oven, about 400°F, allowing 12–15 minutes per pound.

Because the meat is very rich, duck is best served with sharply flavored sauces and fruit, such as oranges, peaches, or cherries. Allow 1 pound of duck per person.

Goose is fattier than chicken and therefore does not need to be barded or basted before cooking. Like duck, goose is best stuffed with herbs, vegetables, or fruit, which are discarded—rather than bread stuffing. Before roasting a young bird, stuff it from the vent end, sprinkle with salt, and bard the bird with any fat taken from its body cavity. Loosely cover the bird with a piece of foil and roast at 400°F, allowing 15 minutes per pound plus an extra 15 minutes. Alternatively, slow-roast the goose near the bottom of the oven at 350°F, allowing 25 minutes per pound. Allow ¾ pound of goose for each person.

Poaching

Rub the surface of a whole bird with lemon juice to preserve the color, and place it in a pan. Add seasonings and enough water to just cover the bird. For every pound of poultry add ½ teaspoon salt. Bring the water to boil and remove any scum from the surface. Reduce the heat to a gentle simmer, then cover with a lid and cook until the bird is tender, about 1–3 hours, depending on age and tenderness. Chicken parts need only 15–20 minutes. Lift the chicken from the pan and serve hot or cold. Use the cooking liquid to make sauce.

Steaming

Place the trussed but unstuffed chicken on a wire rack over a deep pot of boiling water. Cover chicken with foil and steam for 3–4 hours, adding more water when necessary. Let the chicken cool. Remove the skin from the cooked chicken and use the flesh in various low-calorie recipes.

Braising

Lightly sauté a whole bird or parts in a little butter until golden. Remove the bird from the pan and sauté about 1 pound of cleaned, coarsely chopped vegetables, such as carrots, onions, celery, and turnips, in the butter. Replace the poultry on the bed of vegetables and cover the pan tightly with a lid. Cook over low heat on top of the stove or in a 325°F oven until tender. Braising is a slow process, taking up to 2 hours, but cooking time depends on the size and age of the bird.

Duck can be disjointed and braised for about 1 hour in a preheated 350°F oven.

Broiling

To prepare a small chicken for broiling, place it on its breast, cut through the backbone, and open the bird out. Flatten the bird with a meat pounder, breaking the joints where necessary.

Brush the bird all over with melted butter and season lightly with salt and freshly ground black pepper. Cook the bird on the broiler pan under moderate heat for 20–30 minutes, turning it frequently.

Sautéing

Brown the chicken pieces quickly in hot fat, then lower the heat, cover, and cook gently until the meat is tender.

Frying

Before frying chicken parts, coat them with Seasoned Flour (see page 28) or with beaten egg and bread crumbs. Place them in a shallow skillet; avoid crowding pieces, or they will steam-cook. Fry in hot fat until brown and tender.

Deep frying

Heat vegetable oil or shortening in a deep fryer to 375°F and cook the coated chicken pieces until tender, and crisp on the outside (10–15 minutes).

Testing for doneness

Meat thermometers are unreliable for testing poultry for doneness: they are likely to touch bone, which throws off the temperature reading. The best test is to take hold of a drumstick and wiggle it gently. The bone will move easily if the meat is tender. Another method is to prick the skin with a fork. If the juices run clear, the poultry is cooked. A thermometer inserted into the meaty part of the upper thigh will read 180–185°F when poultry is done.

Poultry Stuffings

As a rule of thumb, allow ½ cup of stuffing for each pound of poultry. Bread that is too fresh or too finely crumbed will make stuffing pasty. A meaty stuffing helps to keep the flesh of a large bird moist. Never force stuffing into the poultry cavity; extra dressing can be cooked separately in a greased baking dish.

Bread or Cracker Stuffing

In a large saucepan, sauté **1 tablespoon chopped onion** in ¼ **cup butter**. Add **2 cups bread** or **cracker crumbs** and ¼ **cup Poultry Stock** (see page 10) or **water**. Mix well. Add **1 tablespoon chopped parsley** and **a pinch of sage**; season to taste with **salt** and **pepper**.

Herb Stuffing

Add **a pinch each** of **thyme, parsley, marjoram, savory,** and **sage** to **Bread Stuffing**.

Giblet Stuffing

Sauté finely chopped **giblets** lightly in **butter** and add to **Bread Stuffing**.

Mushroom Stuffing

In a large saucepan, sauté **½ pound sliced mushrooms** and **2 tablespoons chopped green pepper** in ½ **cup butter**. Add **3 cups stale bread crumbs, 3 tablespoons chopped parsley,** and **a pinch of rosemary** or **savory**. Season to taste with **salt** and **pepper**.

Celery Stuffing

Sauté **3 stalks of finely chopped celery** in a little **butter** for a few minutes. Stir into **Bread Stuffing**.

Celery-Apricot Stuffing

Add ¾ **cup finely chopped dried apricots** to **Celery Stuffing**.

Apple Stuffing

Make **Bread Stuffing**, substituting **1 tablespoon bacon fat** or **1 slice of finely chopped bacon** for the butter. Blend in **2 finely chopped medium cooking apples**.

Rice Stuffing

In a large saucepan, sauté **1 small, finely chopped onion** in **2 tablespoons butter** until transparent. Add **½ cup long-grain rice** and sauté for 2–3 minutes. Season to taste with **salt** and **pepper**; add **1 cup Poultry Stock** (see page 10) or **water**. Bring to boil, cover, and cook gently until rice is cooked (about 20 minutes).

Sage and Onion Stuffing

Heat **2 cups Poultry Stock** (see page 10) and pour over **6 cups stale bread crumbs**. Mix in **2 beaten eggs**, and set aside. In a medium skillet, sauté **4 chopped onions** lightly in **½ cup butter**. Add **½ cup finely chopped celery**, **½ cup finely chopped parsley**, and **½ cup raisins**. Add to bread crumbs and mix thoroughly. Add **4 teaspoons sage**, and **salt, pepper**, and **nutmeg**, to taste.

Cranberry Stuffing

In a large saucepan, melt **4 tablespoons butter**, and blend in **4 cups stale bread crumbs**. Add **1 cup fresh or canned cranberries**. If using fresh cranberries, add **¼ cup sugar**. Blend in **¼ cup raisins** and **2 teaspoons chopped lemon peel** or **a pinch of cinnamon**. Season to taste with **salt**; add a little **water**, if necessary. Cook gently for about 10 minutes.

Sausage Stuffing No. 1

Mix **½ pound cooked sausage meat** with **Bread Stuffing**.

Sausage Stuffing No. 2

In a medium skillet, sauté **1 finely chopped onion** with **1 pound sausage meat** for 2–3 minutes. Place in a bowl and add **½ cup bread crumbs**; add **salt** and **pepper**, to taste. Add **1 beaten egg** and some **water** to bind the stuffing. Cool.

Veal Forcemeat Stuffing

In a large bowl, blend **1½ cups bread crumbs** with **2 tablespoons melted butter**. Add **1 small finely chopped onion**. In a meat grinder, finely grind **¼ pound lean veal** and **2 slices of lean bacon**; add to the bread crumbs. Season to taste with **salt** and **pepper**; add **1 lightly beaten egg** and enough **Poultry Stock** (see page 10) or **water** to bind the stuffing.

Chestnut Stuffing

Blend **2 tablespoons chopped parsley** with **Veal Forcemeat Stuffing**. Sauté **2 slices of finely chopped bacon** until crisp; drain. Thoroughly mix bacon, **8 ounces chestnut purée**, and the **finely grated rind of 1 lemon** into the stuffing.

Poultry Stock, Gravy, and Sauces

Chicken or turkey stock is the basis of many gravies, soups, and sauces. It is best made from a fresh, meaty bird. For a dark broth, first brown the meat and bones. Stock freezes well.

Poultry (Chicken or Turkey) Stock

Into a stockpot, put **1 poultry carcass**, broken in pieces, and the following vegetables, all coarsely chopped: **2 medium carrots, 2 stalks of celery**, and **1 onion** or **leek**. Season with **salt** and **pepper**. Cover with **cold water**, and simmer, uncovered, for 4–5 hours, skimming occasionally. Do not boil. Remove the carcass and vegetables; strain the broth. Cool, uncovered, before refrigerating or freezing. Remove fat before using.

Clarified Stock

Blend **1 slightly beaten egg white** with its **shell**, broken, into **1 quart cooled, degreased Poultry Stock** (above). Slowly bring the stock to simmer, without stirring. As a crusty foam accumulates, push it carefully to the side of the pan to make a small opening; watch the soup through this opening to ensure it does not boil. Simmer 10–15 minutes; remove from stove. Set aside for about 20 minutes. Spoon soup carefully from the pan, without disturbing the foam, and strain through a wet cloth bag or a strainer lined with cheesecloth. Cool, uncovered.

Clarified Jellied Consommé

Lightly beat **1 egg white** with **1 tablespoon cold water** in a small bowl. Pour **2 cups cold Poultry Stock** (above) into a medium saucepan, and add egg white. Bring to boil, stirring constantly. Cover, and boil for 5 minutes. Strain through a thick, dampened cheesecloth. Soften **2 tablespoons gelatin** in **4 tablespoons cold water**, and add to the hot—but not boiling—broth. Stir; cool.

Thick Gravy

Remove meat and juices from roasting pan, leaving about **2 tablespoons fat** in the pan. Stir in **1 tablespoon flour**. Cook until mixture thickens and browns. Slowly stir in **1 cup hot Poultry Stock** (above). Season with **salt and pepper**, to taste. Poultry gravy can also be made in a heavy saucepan; butter can be substituted for the poultry fat.

Giblet Gravy

While roast is cooking, add **poultry neck and giblets** (heart and gizzard) to a large saucepan, with **1 small, chopped onion** and **1 chopped stalk of celery**. Cover with **cold water** and simmer for 1 hour. Strain broth, discarding vegetables. Chop giblets fine. Prepare **Thick Gravy** (above), substituting giblet broth for **Poultry Stock**. Add giblets to gravy and heat through a few minutes before serving.

White Sauces

Milk-based sauces vary in consistency, from the gravy-like **White Sauce No. 1** to the binding cream, **White Sauce No. 4**. Cooking procedures are the same for each; only the proportion of butter and flour to milk are different. The recipe below makes 1 cup of sauce.

No. 1 1 tablespoon butter, 1 tablespoon flour, 1 cup milk
No. 2 2 tablespoons butter, 2 tablespoons flour, 1 cup milk
No. 3 3 tablespoons butter, 3 tablespoons flour, 1 cup milk
No. 4 4 tablespoons butter, 4 tablespoons flour, 1 cup milk

Melt **butter** in the upper part of a double boiler. When transparent, add **flour** all at once. Cook mixture directly over medium heat, stirring constantly until it becomes frothy. Do not let it brown. Return to double boiler. Pour in **cold milk**; stir with a whisk until the sauce thickens. Season to taste with **salt** and **pepper**.

Veloutée Sauce

Substitute **Poultry Stock** (see page 10) for milk in **White Sauce No. 1**.

Supreme Sauce

In a small bowl, beat together **2 egg yolks** and **2 tablespoons heavy cream**. Blend into **1 cup Veloutée Sauce** (above) and heat in a medium saucepan without boiling. Cut **2 tablespoons butter** into pieces and add to the sauce.

Brown Sauce

Melt **¼ cup butter** and **½ cup shortening** in a heavy saucepan. Add **¾ cup flour**, and stir constantly over medium–low heat until the mixture is brown. Add **1 coarsely chopped carrot, 1 coarsely chopped onion,** and **1 stalk of sliced celery**. Add **1 sprig of parsley, coarsely chopped**. Brown lightly. Add **1 minced clove of garlic** and **4 cups Poultry Stock** (see page 10). Simmer for 20 minutes. Strain. Cook for 30 more minutes, skimming often.

Tomato Sauce

In a skillet over medium heat, melt **¼ cup butter**. Add **¼ cup flour**. Cook until slightly brown. Add **1 chopped onion** and **½ cup diced celery**; sauté until lightly brown. Stir in **4 cups tomatoes** (canned or fresh), **Bouquet Garni** (see page 110), and **salt** and **pepper**, to taste. Simmer for 1 hour. Strain. Add a pinch of sugar if sauce is too acidic.

Tomato Brown Sauce

In a large saucepan, melt together **¼ cup butter** with **½ cup shortening**; add **¾ cup flour**. Brown over medium heat, stirring constantly. Add the following vegetables, coarsely chopped: **1 carrot, 1 onion, 1 stalk of celery,** and **1 sprig of parsley**. Cook until they start to change color. Add **4 cups Poultry Stock** (see page 10), **1 minced clove of garlic**, and a small amount of **tomato paste**. Cook slowly for 20 minutes. Strain. Cook for 30 more minutes, skimming often.

Asparagus-Chicken Casserole

This tasty creation lends itself well to springtime. (Asparagus is in season from late April to early June.) The dish may be prepared in advance and refrigerated.

Servings   6

Total Time   ⧖

Major Utensils   Large, shallow casserole
Medium saucepan

Ingredients
1½ pounds asparagus, cut in 1-inch pieces
3 cups cooked chicken, cubed
½ cup butter
¼ cup flour
1½ teaspoons salt
¼ teaspoon pepper
¼ teaspoon dry mustard
¼ teaspoon paprika
1 cup light cream
1 cup Chicken Stock (see page 10)
¼ cup pimento, chopped
½ cup almonds, blanched and slivered

Step by Step
1. Steam-cook **asparagus** until barely tender (about 5 minutes).
2. Spread cooked asparagus in bottom of buttered casserole. Sprinkle **chicken** on top. Set aside while making sauce.
3. Melt **butter** in saucepan and add **flour, salt, pepper, mustard,** and **paprika.** Stir constantly over medium heat until sauce bubbles.
4. Remove from heat; add **Chicken Stock** and **cream.** Return to stove and cook, stirring, until it comes to boil and is thickened and smooth.
5. Add **pimento.** Pour over chicken and asparagus. Sprinkle with **almonds.** Bake at 350°F until sauce bubbles (about 30 minutes).

Avocado-Chicken Casserole

Avocados are in season all year-round, which gives this tempting casserole additional flexibility. You can store ripe avocados directly in the refrigerator for a short period of time.

Servings 6

Total Time ⏳ ⏳

Major Utensils Large skillet
Deep casserole

Ingredients
6 chicken breasts, boned (see page 5), or 6 leg and thigh pieces
5 tablespoons flour
1 teaspoon salt
Pepper
¼ teaspoon thyme
1 lemon: grated rind and juice
6 tablespoons butter
2 onions, sliced
1 cup dry white wine
½ cup Chicken Stock (see page 10)
½ cup cream
2 avocados, sliced
1-2 tablespoons oil

Step by Step
1. Coat **chicken** pieces in **4 tablespoons of flour** to which **salt, pepper, thyme**, and **lemon rind** have been added.
2. In a skillet, brown chicken in **4 tablespoons butter.** Place chicken in casserole.
3. In the same skillet, sauté **onion slices** (until soft) in **remaining butter**.
4. Combine **remaining flour** with **Chicken Stock**. Add to onions. Add **white wine**. Bring to boil and cook until thickened.
5. Pour sauce over chicken and bake at 350°F until meat is tender (about 50 minutes).
6. Remove from oven and cool slightly. Turn off heat. Stir in **cream**. Sprinkle **avocados** with **lemon juice**. Place on top of chicken and brush with **oil**. Return to oven for 10 minutes and serve.

Barbecued Chicken

Known familiarly as Chicken BBQ, broiled chicken pieces coated with a piquant herb sauce are quick to prepare and unfailingly popular among all age groups. To vary this recipe, marinate chicken in Garlic Barbecue Sauce (below) before broiling.

Servings	2
Total Time	⏳
Major Utensil	Broiling pan
Ingredients	**1 small chicken, cut in half (see page 7)**
Barbecue Sauce	½ cup **vegetable oil** 1 tablespoon **prepared mustard** ½ teaspoon **thyme** ½ teaspoon **rosemary** ½ teaspoon **fennel** ½ teaspoon **parsley** **Salt and pepper**
Step by Step	**1.** Place **chicken** halves on a well-greased broiling pan, skin side up. **2.** Make barbecue sauce by blending the **oil, mustard, thyme, rosemary, fennel,** and **parsley** in a small bowl. **3.** Brush chicken with the sauce. Broil about 4½–5 inches below the burner for about 20 minutes, basting 2–3 times. Turn chicken over and cook for another 20 minutes, basting several times. **4.** Before serving, season with **salt** and **pepper** to taste.

🍲🍲🍲 Garlic Barbecue Sauce

Blend **5 crushed garlic cloves** with **1 tablespoon lemon juice**, adding a dash of **salt** and **pepper**. Let the mixture stand briefly before rubbing it onto the chicken. Marinate the chicken in a blend of **½ cup vegetable oil** and **6 tablespoons lemon juice** for at least one hour.

Boer Chicken Pie

Tailor-made for big appetites, this dish goes well with buttered new potatoes and beans or peas.

Servings	8
Total Time	⏳⏳⏳
Major Utensils	Stockpot with cover Large baking dish Medium saucepan
Ingredients	2 small chickens, quartered (see page 4) 4 cups water 4 teaspoons salt 1 teaspoon whole allspice 1 teaspoon peppercorns 3 bay leaves 3 medium carrots 10 parsley sprigs 3 celery stalks 3 medium onions, quartered ¼ pound cooked ham, sliced, then quartered 4 hard-cooked eggs, sliced ¼ cup butter ¼ cup flour ⅓ cup sherry 2 tablespoons lemon juice ¼ teaspoon mace ¼ teaspoon pepper 2 egg yolks, beaten until smooth Pie pastry (see page 75) 1 egg, beaten until smooth
Step by Step	**1.** Bring **chicken** to boil in a large pot with **water, 3 teaspoons salt, allspice, peppercorns,** and **bay leaves.** Add **carrots, parsley, celery,** and **onion.** Simmer, covered, until tender (about 30 minutes). **2.** Remove chicken and vegetables; strain broth. Skin and bone chicken; cut meat into chunks. Slice carrots and celery. Place in a greased baking dish. Top with **ham** and **eggs**; set aside. **3.** Melt the **butter** in a saucepan. Stir in **flour**; gradually add 2 cups of the strained broth, **sherry, lemon juice, mace, remaining salt,** and **pepper.** Cook over medium-low heat, stirring until thickened. Stir in **egg yolks.** Simmer, stirring, until thickened. **4.** Pour sauce over chicken. Cover dish with **pie pastry.** Cut vents for steam; brush with **beaten egg.** Bake at 425°F until golden (about 30 minutes).

Chicken and Pork Pie

This pie is substantial enough to serve alone, although peas or broccoli help round out the meal.

Servings	6
Total Time	⏳ ⏳ ⏳
Major Utensils	Stockpot with cover Deep skillet with cover Casserole
Ingredients	1 large chicken, cut in pieces (see page 4) 1 onion, studded with 1 clove 1 stalk of celery 1 carrot, sliced 1 sprig of parsley 1 bay leaf Thyme Marjoram 2 pounds lean ground pork Salt and pepper 1 large onion, chopped 2 cloves of garlic, crushed Nutmeg 1 cup Brown Sauce (see page 11) Rich Pie Pastry (see page 69)
Step by Step	**1.** Place **chicken** in stockpot with the **studded onion, celery, carrot, parsley, bay leaf,** a pinch each of **thyme** and **marjoram,** and **salt.** Cover with cold water, bring to boil, and simmer until meat is tender (about 30 minutes). Cool in broth. Strain, reserving chicken and broth. **2.** In a greased skillet over medium heat, sauté **pork** until it loses color. Add **salt, pepper, chopped onion, garlic,** a pinch each of **thyme** and **nutmeg,** and just enough chicken broth to cover meat. Cover and simmer for 1 hour 30 minutes. Cool; skim fat. **3.** Bone chicken, and cut meat into large chunks. Combine with pork, and adjust seasoning. Stir in **Brown Sauce.** Place in the casserole, and cover with **Rich Pie Pastry.** Seal edges, cut vents, and bake at 350°F until **crust** is golden.

Index

Almond(s). *See* Nuts
Almond dressing, 41
Apple(s)
  orchard, duck in the, 109
  stuffing, 8
Artichokes, mushroom-chicken with, 83
Asparagus-chicken casserole, 12
Aspic
  basic jelly, 27
  smoked turkey in, 124
  turkey-cranberry, 132
Avocado-chicken casserole, 13
Bacon
  chicken brochettes, 24
  chicken Maryland, 44
  duck pâté, 104
Banana(s)
  chicken Maryland, 44
Basic jelly aspic, 27
Bean sprouts
  turkey chop suey, 131
Beef, ground
  spicy turkey meat loaf, 128
Beer batter, 74
  deep-fried chicken, 74
Beurre manié, 56
Blanched salt pork, 21
Boiled rice, 70
Bouquet garni, 110
Bread(s)
  chicken livers with grapes, 101
  croutons, 127
  garlic croutons, 58
  or cracker stuffing, 8
  turkey balls, 130
Broccoli, turkey with, 140
Broiled tomatoes, 81
Brown sauce, 11
Butter(s)
  beurre manié, 56
  chicken Kiev, 37
  chicken log, 42
  chicken liver pâté, 100
  clarified, 22
  garlic, 137
  spread, 48
Catsup, 128
  sugarless, 66
Celery
  -apricot stuffing, 8
  curried chicken salad, 73
  stuffing, 8
  turkey-cranberry aspic, 132
Cheese(s)
  chicken log, 42
  chicken cordon-bleu, 28
  chicken breasts Milano, 23
  chicken Torcello, 55
  pastry, 45

Roquefort chicken, 93
turkey scallops cordon-bleu, 135
turkey scallops Mirabel, 136
Chestnut stuffing, 9
Chicken coating mix, 78
Chicken stock, 10
Clarified butter, 22
Clarified stock, 10
Coconut milk, guinea hen with, 119
Consommé, clarified jellied, 10
Cooked poultry
  asparagus-chicken casserole, 12
  chicken croquettes, 29
  chicken log, 42
  chicken salad, 49
  curried chicken salad, 73
  miniature chicken balls, 82
  oyster-chicken casserole, 87
  quick chicken casserole, 92
  spinach and turkey pie, 129
  turkey balls, 130
  turkey-cranberry aspic, 132
  turkey hash, 133
  turkey potpie, 134
  turkey soufflé with olives, 137
Corn fritters
  chicken Maryland, 44
Cornstarch thickening, 122
Cranberries
  cranberry stuffing, 9
  turkey-cranberry aspic, 132
Cream(s)
  asparagus-chicken casserole, 12
  chicken breasts in sherry, 22
  chicken Tetrazzini, 52
  chicken with sour, 63
  duck in wine sauce, 106
  guinea hen with coconut milk, 119
Crêpes
  à la king, 68
  Peking duck, 114–115
Croutons. *See* Bread(s)
Curry
  curried chicken, 70
  curried chicken salad, 73
Duck pâté, 104
Duck with olives, 112
Dumplings, 32
  chicken hot pot, 32
Eggs
  Boer chicken pie, 15
  smoked turkey in aspic, 124
  turkey soufflé with olives, 137
Eggplant
  chicken Provence style, 47

guinea hen Arlésienne, 118
sautéed, 118
Endive(s), Belgian
  chicken salad, 49
French dressing, 49
Fried onion rings, 73
Garlic
  butter, 137
  chicken with, 58
  barbecue sauce, 14
  croutons, 58
Giblet
  gravy, 10
  stock, 105
  stuffing, 8
Glaze. *See* Sauce(s)
Gooseberries, goose with, 117
Grapefruit
  chicken brochettes, 24
Grapes, chicken livers with, 101
Gravy. *See* Sauce(s)
Green peas
  duck with, 110
  paella, 88
  turkey potpie, 134
Ham
  Boer chicken pie, 15
  chicken Antonia, 19
  chicken cordon-bleu, 28
  chicken jambalaya, 34
  guinea hen with cognac, 120
  spiced chicken and rice, 94–95
  spinach and turkey pie, 129
  turkey scallops cordon-bleu, 135
Herb stuffing, 8
Italian seasoning, 23
Jellied consommé. *See* Consommé, clarified jellied, 10
Leek(s)
  braised turkey roll, 122
Leftovers. *See* Cooked poultry
Lemon-chicken Catalan, 81
Lemony turkey kabobs, 123
Light chicken stock, 10
Liqueur. *See* Brandy and liqueur
Litchi nuts, guinea hen with, 121
Livers, chicken
  pâté, 100
  sweet and sour, 102
  with grapes, 101
Mashed potatoes, 39
Mayonnaise, 42
  chicken log, 42
  curried chicken salad, 73
  turkey-cranberry aspic, 132
Milk
  coconut, 119

oven-poached creamy
  chicken, 86
Mornay sauce, 68
Mushroom(s)
  chicken cacciatore, 25
  chicken flambé with cream,
    30
  chicken Tetrazzini, 52
  chicken wings with, 57
  chicken with, 59
  chicken with artichokes, 83
  chicken with sour cream, 63
  coq au vin, 67
  duck in wine sauce, 106
  lemony turkey kabobs, 123
  stuffing, 8
Noodles. See Pasta and
  noodles
Nuts
  almond dressing, 41
  chicken log, 42
  crunchy almond chicken, 69
  curried chicken salad, 73
  orange-glazed chicken, 84
Oriental chicken, 85
Okra, chicken stew with, 51
Olives
  duck with, 112
  smoked turkey in aspic, 124
  turkey soufflé with, 137
Onion(s)
  and sage stuffing, 9
  chicken with orange and, 60
  rings, fried, 73
Onions, pearl
  chicken flambé with cream,
    30
  chicken in red wine, 33
  coq au vin, 67
  duck in wine sauce, 106
  duck with green peas, 110
  duck with turnip or olives,
    112
Orange(s)
  and onion, chicken with, 60
  curried chicken salad, 73
  duck breasts in pastry, 104
  glaze, 84
  -glazed chicken, 84
  golden glazed broilers, 79
  goose with gooseberries, 117
  Hungarian chicken, 80
  sauce
    duck in orange, 105
    goose in orange, 116
    zucchini-chicken with, 99
Oyster-chicken casserole, 87
Parmesan cheese. See
  Cheeses(s)
Pasta and noodles
  chicken lasagna, 38
  chicken Tetrazzini, 52
  chicken Torcello, 55
  Chinese chicken casserole,
    65
  quick chicken casserole, 92

spaghetti with turkey sauce,
  127
Pastry and pies
  Boer chicken pie, 15
  cheese pastry, 45
    chicken pie with, 45
    turkey potpie, 134
  chicken and pork pie, 16
  pie pastry, 75
  puff pastry
    duck breasts in, 104
  rich pie pastry, 69
  spinach and turkey pie, 129
Peaches, duck with, 111
Pearl onions. See Onions, pearl
Peas. See Green peas
Pie pastry, 75
Pineapple
  -chicken casserole, 91
  turkey-cranberry aspic, 132
Pork
  chicken and pork pie, 16
  chicken ballottine, 20–21
  chicken legs chaud-froid,
    40–41
  salt pork
    chicken in red wine, 33
  salt pork, blanched, 21
    chicken ballottine, 20–21
    chicken in red wine, 33
    chicken with sautéed
      vegetables, 62
    coq au vin, 67
    duck with green peas, 110
    turkey scallops Mirabel, 136
Potatoes
  chicken poached with, 46
  mashed, 39
  stuffing, 139
  turkey hash, 133
  turkey stuffed with, 138–139
Poultry seasoning, 134
Poultry stock, 10
Prepared shrimp, 34
Rice
  boiled, 70
  chicken jambalaya, 34
  chicken Madrid, 43
  pilaf, 61
    chicken wings with
      mushrooms, 57
    chicken with, 61
  paella, 88
  spiced chicken and, 94–95
  stuffing, 9
  wild
    Roquefort chicken, 93
Rich pie pastry, 69
Sage and onion stuffing, 9
Sauce(s)
  barbecue, 14
  brown, 11
    chicken and pork pie, 16
    chicken cacciatore, 25
    chicken with sautéed
      vegetables, 62

coq au vin, 67
duck with green peas, 110
duck with peaches, 111
duck with turnip or olives,
  112
guinea hen with cognac,
  120
guinea hen with litchi nuts,
  121
mushroom-chicken and
  artichokes, 83
turkey scallops Mirabel,
  136
zucchini-chicken with
  orange, 99
chaud-froid, 26–27, 40–41
cream
  chicken fricassee, 31
glazes
  Chinese deviled chicken,
    66
  deviled chicken, 75
  golden glazed broilers, 79
  orange, 84
  sugar-broiled chicken, 96
  teriyaki chicken, 98
gravy
  giblet, 10
  thick, 10
Mirabel, turkey scallops, 136
Mornay, 68
crêpes à la king, 68
orange
  duck in, 105
  goose in, 116
sherry, 22
supreme, 11
  chicken with rice pilaf, 61
sweet and sour, 102
tomato, 11
  turkey scallops Mirabel,
    136
tomato brown, 11
  chicken Provence style, 47
velouté, 11
  crêpes à la king, 68
white
  chicken flambé with
    cream, 30
  chicken sauté with
    Madeira, 50
  oyster-chicken casserole,
    87
  quick chicken casserole,
    92
white, 11
  chicken croquettes, 29
  curried chicken, 70
  miniature chicken balls, 82
Sausage
  Cornish hen with, 103
  paella, 88
  stuffing, 9
Sautéed eggplant, 118
Seafood
  oyster-chicken casserole, 87

Chicken Antonia

The tempting sauce that accompanies this vegetable-rich dish is flavored with dry port wine.

Servings	4
Total Time	⌛
Major Utensil	Large, deep skillet with cover
Ingredients	1 small chicken, cut in pieces (see page 4)
	3 tablespoons olive oil
	2 carrots, thinly sliced
	2 onions, finely chopped
	4 stalks of celery, diced
	3 slices of ham, diced
	1 green or red pepper, cut in slivers
	½ pound mushrooms
	2 teaspoons cornstarch
	½ teaspoon curry powder
	1 teaspoon paprika
	Salt and pepper
	1 cup Chicken Stock (see page 10)
	3 tablespoons dry port wine
Step by Step	**1.** In a skillet, brown **chicken pieces, carrots, onions, celery**, and **ham** in **olive oil** over medium heat.
	2. Add **green** or **red pepper** slivers and **mushrooms**. Sprinkle with **cornstarch, curry powder,** and **paprika**. **Salt** lightly and add a dash of **pepper**.
	3. Add the **Chicken Stock**. Cook while stirring until the liquid starts to boil. Cover and cook over very low heat until the chicken is tender (30 to 45 minutes).
	4. Stir the **port** into the sauce, cook for 1 minute, and serve.

Chicken Ballottine

Ballottine *is a French culinary term for a dish of whole poultry that has been boned and stuffed. Traditional* ballottines *require the chicken to be poached, pressed beneath heavy weights, and coated with aspic. This is a far simpler version: the boned and stuffed chicken is roasted. If this dish is to be served hot, prepare a gravy from the pan juices.*

Servings	6
Total Time	⏳ ⏳ ⏳
Major Utensils	Small skillet
	Shallow roasting pan
Ingredients	1 large chicken
	1 onion, chopped
	2 tablespoons butter
	2 tablespoons oil
	1 pound ground veal
	1 pound ground pork
	2 cloves of garlic, crushed
	Salt and pepper
	Poultry Seasoning (see page 134)
	1 egg
	2 slices of cooked ham, ¼ inch thick, cut in strips
	½ pound Blanched Salt Pork (see page 21), cut in strips
	1 pork tenderloin
	Stuffed olives
	Shortening
	Chicken Stock (see page 10) or water
	Thick Gravy (see page 10)

Step by Step

1. Sauté **onion** lightly in **butter** and **oil** until transparent but not colored. Set aside to cool.

2. Combine in a large mixing bowl the **veal, pork, garlic, salt, pepper, Poultry Seasoning,** and **egg.** Add onion.

3. Using a boning knife, bone the **chicken** as follows:
- Cut skin around tips of drumsticks and, without tearing the skin, free meat from drumstick bones. Cut around thigh joints, leaving skin intact.
- Remove wing at joint. Slit skin on back from neck to rump. Continue boning in the following order: wings, back, upper thighs, and breast. Remove tendons from breast and legs.

4. Turn the chicken skin side up, and sew the openings at wings and thighs, stitching as follows:
- Push needle downward through skin. Pull through, leaving a fairly long tail of thread so that it will be easier to remove once the ballottine is cooked; do not knot.

Step by Step Continued

- Push needle back upward through the skin on the same side of the opening, and pull thread through.
- Repeat the procedure on the opposite side of the opening.
- Stitch in this manner until the opening is closed.

5. Place chicken flat, skin side down. Spoon half the stuffing into the center of the bird. Alternating, lay half the strips of **ham** and **Blanched Salt Pork** on the stuffing. Place **pork tenderloin** in the center, and add more ham and pork strips and **olives.** Cover with the remaining stuffing.

6. Close chicken, and sew to shape the ballottine, using the technique described in Step 4. Truss crosswise with string every 2 inches; truss once lengthwise to enhance the shape of the ballottine.

7. In a shallow roasting pan, melt **shortening.** Place ballottine in the pan and brush it with the melted shortening. Season with **salt** and **pepper.**

8. Place ballottine in a preheated 350°F oven. After the first 5 minutes, move the ballottine to prevent it from sticking to the pan. Roast for about 3 hours, basting frequently with pan juices. Add shortening after about 15 minutes to prevent the pan juices from burning. If the ballotine is browning too quickly, cover it lightly with aluminum foil.

9. Chicken is done if juices run clear when meat is pricked with a metal skewer. Remove from oven. Cut string with scissors, and pull out string and thread.

10. Add **Chicken Stock** or **water** to pan, and scrape. To recover juice for **Thick Gravy,** pour liquid into a heatproof cup or steep-sided bowl. Let stand, then skim off the layer of fat that rises to the top.

11. If the ballottine is prepared ahead of time and frozen, thaw before cooking. (Leftovers may also be sliced, frozen, and thawed as needed.)

♦♦♦ Blanched Salt Pork

The purpose of blanching salt pork is to remove some of the salt. Bring **2 quarts water** to boil; add ½ **pound salt pork**. Simmer for 10 minutes; drain.

Chicken Breasts in Sherry

Flambéing *adds a flourish to this simple but elegant dish. Other types of poultry can be substituted for the chicken.*

Servings	6
Total Time	⏳
Major Utensils	Large skillet Small saucepan Small skillet
Ingredients	**6 chicken breasts** **Salt and pepper** **5 tablespoons Clarified Butter (below)**
Sauce	**5 tablespoons whiskey** **½ cup dry sherry** **1 cup light cream** **4 tablespoons Brown Sauce (see page 11)** **2 red peppers, cut into strips** **Butter** **Lemon juice**
Side dish	**Boiled Rice (see page 70)**
Step by Step	**1.** Season **chicken breasts** with **salt** and **pepper**. In a large skillet over high heat, sauté chicken on both sides until golden in **Clarified Butter**. Remove from pan, and keep hot. **2.** To prepare sauce, heat **whiskey** gently in a small saucepan; light it, and pour it flaming into the pan juices. When flames die, add **sherry** and scrape pan. Stir in **cream** and **Brown Sauce**. Cook several minutes. **3.** In a small skillet, sauté strips of **red pepper** in **butter** and **lemon juice**. Add to contents of skillet sauce. **4.** Pour skillet sauce over the chicken breasts before serving with **Boiled Rice**.

❂❂❂ Clarified Butter

Melt butter in a skillet over very low heat. A milky sediment will form, and the clarified butter will rise to the surface, as clear as oil. Carefully pour off this clarified butter into another container.

Chicken Breasts Milano

The accent is Italian in this flavorful creation. The dish can be prepared and refrigerated the day before cooking.

Servings	12
Total Time	⌛ ⌛
Major Utensil	Large baking dish
Ingredients	12 chicken breasts, boned and skinned (see page 5) 2½ cups Bread Stuffing (see page 8) ¼ cup parsley flakes 1 teaspoon salt ½ cup Parmesan cheese, grated 1 tablespoon Italian Seasoning (below) ¾ cup butter, melted ¼ teaspoon garlic salt ½ teaspoon dry mustard ¾ teaspoon Worcestershire sauce
Step by Step	**1.** Mix **Bread Stuffing, parsley, salt, Parmesan cheese,** and **Italian Seasoning** in a pie or cake pan. Set aside. **2.** Mix **butter, garlic salt, mustard,** and **Worcestershire sauce** in a bowl. **3.** Dip **chicken breasts** in butter mixture, then coat with crumb mixture. **4.** Roll up, fasten with toothpicks, and place in buttered baking dish. Pour remaining butter mixture over top. **5.** Cover with foil. Bake at 325°–350°F for 1 hour. Remove foil and bake 20 minutes longer.

🍲🍲🍲 Italian Seasoning

In a small glass jar, blend **3 tablespoons oregano, 2 tablespoons basil, 1 tablespoon marjoram, 1 tablespoon onion powder**, and **2 teaspoons garlic powder**. Shake jar to blend seasonings. Cover tightly until needed.

Chicken Brochettes

Grapefruit segments and bacon provide a zesty contrast of flavors in this chicken kebab recipe. Marinate the poultry in the morning, then pop it in the broiler or on the barbecue for a fast, delicious evening meal.

Servings	4 to 6
Total Time	⌛ ⌛ ⌛
Major Utensil	Skewers
Ingredients	**1 small chicken, boned and cut in large chunks (see pages 4 and 5)** **2 grapefruit: juice reserved from ½ grapefruit; remainders peeled and divided in segments** **½ cup vegetable oil** **½ pound bacon, cut in large chunks** **1 tablespoon paprika** **Salt and pepper**
Step by Step	**1.** Blend the **grapefruit juice** with the **oil**. Marinate the **chicken** pieces in this mixture for 6 hours at room temperature. **2.** Thread **bacon** chunks, chicken pieces, and **grapefruit segments** on skewers. Dust with **salt, pepper,** and **paprika**. **3.** Grill on a barbecue or in a broiler at least 5 inches below the burner, turning several times, until chicken is lightly browned (about 10 minutes on each side).

Because poultry is a dry meat, it must be broiled carefully. Place thin pieces close to the burner so they do not dry out. Thicker pieces should be cooked farther from the heat source, lest their surfaces brown too quickly. Marinades and basting sauces help preserve meat juices.

Chicken Cacciatore

Also known as Hunter-style Chicken, the preparation of this popular recipe is based on a method of cooking game in the wild, during a shoot. The term cacciatore indicates a meat dish cooked with mushrooms, green onions, and white wine.

Servings	6 to 8
Total Time	⏳ ⏳
Major Utensils	Large, ovenproof skillet with cover Small saucepan
Ingredients	**2 small chickens, skinned and cut in pieces (see pages 4 and 5)** **Salt and pepper** **¼ cup butter** **¼ cup oil** **¼ cup brandy** **1 pound small mushrooms, stems removed** **2 green onions, finely chopped** **4 tomatoes, blanched and peeled, or 1 medium can tomatoes, drained** **1 cup white wine** **½ cup Chicken Stock (see page 10)** **1 cup Brown Sauce (see page 11)** **Parsley or tarragon**
Step by Step	**1.** Season **chicken** pieces with **salt** and **pepper.** Sauté in **butter and oil** in a skillet over medium heat until browned. **2.** Heat **brandy** gently in a small saucepan; ignite it, and pour it flaming over chicken. When flaming stops, remove chicken from pan and keep hot. **3.** Add more butter and oil to pan, if necessary. Sauté the **mushrooms** lightly with **green onions.** **4.** Cut **tomatoes** into large chunks, add to mushrooms, and cook for a few minutes. **5.** Stir **wine, Chicken Stock,** and **Brown Sauce** into vegetables. Adjust seasoning. **6.** Return chicken to the skillet. Cover, and bake at 350°F until chicken is tender (about 1 hour). **7.** Serve sprinkled with **parsley** or **tarragon.**

Chicken Chaud-Froid

The French culinary term chaud-froid refers to an elaborate dish of meat, poultry, game, or fish that is coated with a cream sauce and glazed with aspic. In this recipe, tender chicken breasts are decorated with peels of cucumber and lemon rinds as well as strips of tomato and green pepper before the aspic is applied. Chicken Chaud-froid is served cold. Salad and French bread go well with it.

Servings 6

Total Time ⏳ ⏳ ⏳

Major Utensils Large saucepan with cover
Medium saucepan
Wire rack

Ingredients 6 chicken breasts
1 large onion: cut in 2 pieces, 1 inch from end
1 sprig of thyme
1 small bay leaf
1 small carrot, scraped
6 parsley sprigs
6 peppercorns
¼ teaspoon salt
1 cup milk
2 tablespoons unsalted butter
2 tablespoons flour
Salt and pepper
1 tablespoon unflavored gelatin
3 tablespoons cold, Clarified Stock (see page 10)

Garnish 1 large tomato, cut in narrow strips
1 small green pepper, cut in narrow strips
1-inch piece of cucumber peel, cut in narrow strips
Rind of 1 small lemon, cut in narrow strips
1 cup Basic Jelly Aspic (see page 27)

Step by Step 1. Put the **chicken breasts** in the large saucepan. Add the larger piece of **onion** to the pan together with the **thyme, bay leaf**, and enough cold **water** to cover the chicken. Bring slowly to a boil, remove the scum, and cover the pan. Simmer until the meat is tender (20–25 minutes).

2. Lift out the chicken; drain and set aside, discarding cooking liquid, onion, and herbs.

3. To make the chaud-froid sauce, put the **carrot** in the saucepan with the 1-inch onion slice, **parsley sprigs, peppercorns, salt,** and **milk**. Bring the mixture slowly to boil, then turn off the heat and leave the milk to infuse for 30 minutes. Strain.

Step by Step Continued

- Melt the **butter** in a medium saucepan; stir in the **flour**, and cook for 2 minutes over low heat. Gradually stir in the strained milk. Bring sauce to boil, stirring continuously, and cook gently for 2 minutes. Season to taste with **salt** and **pepper**.
- Soften the **plain gelatin** in the **Clarified Stock,** then gradually add it to the white sauce and stir over low heat until completely dissolved.

4. Meanwhile, remove the skin carefully from the chicken breasts, pat them dry, and place on a wire rack.

5. If the chaud-froid sauce has not cooled and thickened slightly, stir it over cracked ice until it is about to congeal.

6. Coat each chicken breast carefully with the chaud-froid sauce, allowing any excess to run off. Leave for 15 minutes to set.

7. Dip **tomato, pepper,** and **cucumber** and **lemon peel strips** in **Basic Jelly Aspic** and arrange them in decorative patterns on the chicken pieces. Allow the decorations to set.

8. Spoon the remaining aspic over the chicken.

9. Place the chicken in the refrigerator until it has set completely.

Basic Jelly Aspic

In a small saucepan, sprinkle **1 tablespoon unflavored gelatin** on **½ cup cold liquid**. Let stand until gelatin has softened (about 5 minutes). Place pan over very low heat and stir until gelatin dissolves. Remove from heat; add **1¼–1½ cups liquid** (depending on recipe), and stir well.

This recipe is illustrated on page 71.

Chicken Cordon-Bleu

Although it has many imitators, true Gruyère cheese is made only in Switzerland. Used in the recipe below, it lends subtle pungency to this fast dish. Swiss Emmenthal is a good substitute for Gruyère, although its flavor is less sharp.

Servings 4

Total Time ⌛

Major Utensils Medium skillet
Meat mallet

Ingredients
- 4 chicken breasts, boned and skinned (see page 5)
- 4 thin slices of ham
- 4 slices of Gruyère cheese
- ⅓ cup Seasoned Flour (below)
- 1 egg, beaten with
  - 1 tablespoon water
- 1 cup fine, dry bread crumbs
- Vegetable oil for frying

Step by Step

1. Place **chicken breasts** between plastic wrap or wax paper. With a meat mallet, pound to ¼-**inch thickness**.
2. Place 1 slice of **ham** and **Gruyère cheese** on each piece of chicken. Roll up, jelly-roll fashion, and secure with wooden toothpicks.
3. Roll chicken rolls in **Seasoned Flour**. Then dip in the **egg-water** mixture. Finally, roll in **bread crumbs** until thoroughly coated.
4. In the skillet, fry chicken in **2 inches of vegetable oil** until crisp and golden (about 7 minutes), turning often. Drain well before serving.

Seasoned Flour

Combine **1 cup flour, 1 teaspoon salt**, and ¼ **teaspoon black pepper** or ½ **teaspoon paprika**.

Chicken Croquettes

Prepare Chicken Croquettes in advance—and use up leftover poultry. Serve with a thick, piquant sauce alongside. Croquettes should be crispy, never oily.

Servings 6

Total Time ⌛

Major Utensils Medium skillet
Deep fryer

Ingredients
**2 cups cooked chicken, ground
1 onion, chopped
¼ cup celery, chopped
2 tablespoons butter
1 tablespoon parsley
1 teaspoon lemon juice
½-1 cup White Sauce No. 4 (see page 11)
Salt and pepper
Flour
1 egg, beaten
Bread crumbs
Vegetable oil or shortening for deep frying**

Step by Step
1. In a skillet, sauté the **onion** and **celery** lightly in **butter**.
2. Add the ground **chicken, parsley, lemon juice**, and **White Sauce**. Season to taste with **salt and pepper**. Let cool.
3. With floured hands, shape the chicken mixture into croquettes, using about 2 tablespoons of chicken for each oblong.
4. Dredge them in **flour**, dip in the **egg**, then roll in **bread crumbs**. Chill until firm.
5. Heat oil to 375°F in a deep fryer and cook croquettes for a few minutes, until golden.

Chicken Flambé with Cream

Here's a recipe that permits you to cook with style, as you flambé with orange liqueur. It's an excellent meal for a small dinner party.

Servings 6 to 8

Total Time ⏳⏳

Major Utensils Large ovenproof skillet
Small saucepan

Ingredients **2 small chickens, skinned and cut in pieces (see pages 4 and 5)**
Salt and pepper
4 tablespoons butter or
  2 tablespoons butter and 2 tablespoons oil
20 pearl onions
1 pound medium mushrooms
¾ cup orange liqueur (Cointreau)
1⅔ cups dry white wine (½ bottle)
Beurre Manié (see page 56)
4 tablespoons heavy cream

Step by Step **1.** Season the **chicken pieces** well with **salt and pepper.** In the skillet, sauté the chicken in **butter,** or **butter and oil,** over medium heat until browned.
2. Add **onions** and whole **mushrooms** to the pan, and sauté lightly.
3. Bake at 350°F for about 30 minutes.
4. Heat **orange liqueur** gently in a saucepan; ignite it and pour it flaming over the chicken and vegetables.
5. When flames die down, add **wine.** Bake for 15 minutes.
6. Remove chicken from the pan; set aside and keep hot. Stir the **Beurre Manié** into the pan juices, then add **cream** and simmer for 5 minutes. Adjust seasoning.
7. Return the chicken pieces to the skillet and moisten with the sauce before serving.

As a rule of thumb, use 2 tablespoons of liqueur or brandy for each serving of meat to be flambéed. Heat the liquor until it is warm (never hot) before igniting it. The food to be flamed must be warm as well.

Chicken Fricassee

While boned chicken pieces cook slowly in milk, the carcass is simmering with vegetables to make a broth for the sauce. French cooks add whipped cream just before serving.

Servings   4 to 6

Total Time   ⏳ ⏳

Major Utensils   Ovenproof skillet with cover
Medium saucepan
Small stockpot

Ingredients
1 small chicken: boned and cut into chunks; carcass and some fat saved
2 tablespoons butter
Salt and pepper
1 small onion, finely chopped
Nutmeg, grated
1 cup milk

Cream Sauce
2 tablespoons butter
1 teaspoon chicken fat, diced
4 tablespoons flour
2 cups Light Chicken Stock (below)
Salt and pepper
2-3 tablespoons heavy cream, whipped

Step by Step

1. Prepare **Light Chicken Stock,** using **carcass** from the boned chicken.
2. Meanwhile, melt the **butter** in a skillet over medium heat until golden, then brown **chicken chunks** on all sides. Sprinkle with **salt and pepper,** and add **onion** and a **pinch of nutmeg.**
3. Pour **milk** on top. Bring to simmer, cover tightly, and cook in 250°F oven until chicken is tender (about 1 hour).
4. Pour off milk, strain, and set aside for use in sauce (Step 5).
5. Make the **Cream Sauce** by melting **butter** and **chicken fat** in a saucepan, then adding the **flour.** Stir over low heat for 3 minutes, without browning. Beat in strained milk with a whisk. Add Light Chicken Stock. Beat and stir over medium heat until smooth.
6. Pour sauce over chicken, return pan to burner, and simmer while stirring gently for 1 minute. Season to taste with **salt** and **pepper.** Remove from heat and blend in **whipped cream** just before serving.

🍲🍲🍲 Light Chicken Stock

Place **chicken carcass** in a stockpot with **1 stalk of celery, 1 sliced carrot, 1 bay leaf, 1 teaspoon salt,** and **3 cups water.** Bring to boil, cover, and simmer over low heat for 1 hour. Strain. Measure. Boil to reduce to 2 cups broth.

Chicken Hot Pot

Here's a very simple, no-nonsense recipe that is both tasty and satisfying. It can be prepared with a minimum of effort, and the ingredients permit considerable flexibility.

Servings   4 to 6

Total Time   ⌛ ⌛

Major Utensil   Stockpot

Ingredients
1 small chicken, cut in pieces (see page 4)
Salt and peppercorns
Savory
2 bay leaves
4-6 small, whole potatoes
4-6 large carrots, sliced
3 medium onions, sliced
Dumplings (below)

Step by Step

1. Place **chicken** in stockpot; add enough water to cover.

2. Bring to boil and skim off any scum. Add **salt, peppercorns** and **savory** to taste. Add **bay leaves** and **onions**.

3. Simmer 1 hour, then add **potatoes** and **carrots**; simmer again for 1 hour.

4. Meanwhile, prepare **Dumplings**. Add to hot pot 15 minutes before meal is to be served.

🍲🍲🍲 Dumplings

Blend **1½ cups unsifted flour, 1 tablespoon baking powder,** and **½ teaspoon salt** in a mixing bowl. Add **¼ cup vegetable shortening.** Blend with a fork until mixture is moist and crumbly. Add **cold water** to bind. Drop by the tablespoonful into the stew and let simmer for 15 minutes.

Chicken in Red Wine

Straightforward and easy, this gourmet dish bears a distinct resemblance to the French classic, Coq au vin, *yet takes less time to prepare. In as few as 20 minutes the chicken is in the pot, simmering.*

Servings	4
Total Time	⏳ ⏳
Major Utensils	Deep skillet with cover Small saucepan Small skillet
Ingredients	**1 small chicken, cut in pieces (see page 4)** **¾ cup salt pork, diced** **6 tablespoons butter** **Salt and pepper** **16 pearl onions** **6 tablespoons brandy** **1 bottle red wine** **½ cup Chicken Stock (see page 10)** **Bouquet Garni (see page 110)** **2 cloves of garlic, crushed** **¼ pound mushrooms** **4 tablespoons flour**
Garnish	**Parsley sprigs**
Step by Step	**1.** Render the **salt pork** in **2 tablespoons butter** in the deep skillet. Season the **chicken pieces** to taste with **salt and pepper**. Remove the salt pork from the pan and slowly brown the chicken in the fat over gentle heat. **2.** Add the **onions** to the skillet, together with the rendered pork; turn the onions until they are glazed. **3.** Warm **brandy** in a small saucepan, pour it over the chicken; set alight. As soon as flames have died down, pour in **wine** and **Chicken Stock**; add the **Bouquet Garni** and **garlic**. Bring to boil. Check seasoning, cover, and simmer for 30 minutes. **4.** Meanwhile, sauté the **mushrooms** in **2 tablespoons butter** and drain. Add to the chicken after it has simmered for 30 minutes. Cover and cook until chicken is tender (about 10 more minutes). Transfer chicken and vegetables to a heated serving dish and keep warm. **5.** To make the sauce, reduce pan liquid by boiling to about 2 cups. Blend **flour** and **remaining butter** into a paste. Remove pan from heat; beat in small balls of paste until sauce thickens. Return to stove and bring slowly to boil. **6.** Pour sauce over the chicken and garnish with **parsley**.

This recipe is illustrated on page 17.

Chicken Jambalaya

This Creole-style dish follows a tradition of cooking that originated in New Orleans. It combines shrimp and ham with chicken and a variety of seasonings.

Servings	4 to 6
Total Time	⌛
Major Utensil	Large, deep skillet with cover
Ingredients	1 small chicken, cut in pieces (see page 4) ½ pound ham, finely diced ½ pound raw, shelled Prepared Shrimp (below) ¼ cup oil or butter ⅓ cup onion, minced 1 clove of garlic, minced 1 cup stewed tomatoes 1 bay leaf ¼ teaspoon thyme ½ cup celery, diced 1 green pepper, diced 1 cup rice ¼ cup parsley, chopped
Step by Step	**1.** Brown **ham** lightly in **oil** or **butter** in skillet. Stir in **onion** and **garlic** and sauté until soft. Add **chicken** and **shrimp**. **2.** In mixing bowl, combine **stewed tomatoes, bay leaf,** and **thyme**. Pour over ham and chicken. Simmer 30 minutes. **3.** Stir in **celery, green pepper,** and **rice**. (Add water to cover rice, if necessary.) **4.** Simmer, covered, until chicken and rice are tender (about 30 more minutes). Remove bay leaf. Sprinkle with **chopped parsley** before serving.

🍎🍎🍎 Prepared Shrimp

Shrimp may be deveined before or after cooking. It may be served shelled (peeled) or not, depending on the recipe, although it is always deveined. Remove the blackish vein with the point of a small, sharp knife, then wash shrimp under cold running water. To cook, simmer in salted water for 1–3 minutes, depending on size. Shrimp will be reddish and curled when done.

Chicken Kiev

Simple to prepare, these buttery, slightly garlicky breasts of chicken can dress up family meals as well as make impressive guest fare. Preparation is done well ahead of time, and the final product gets from fridge to table in only 7 minutes.

Servings   4

Total Time   ⏳ ⏳ ⏳

Major Utensils   Meat mallet
Deep fryer

Ingredients   4 chicken breasts, skinned and boned (see page 5)
¼ cup butter
1 clove of garlic, minced
2 tablespoons fresh parsley, chopped
Seasoned Flour (see page 28)
2 eggs, beaten lightly with 1 tablespoon water
4 slices of fresh bread, finely crumbed
Oil for deep frying

Step by Step   **1.** Cream **butter** with **garlic** and **parsley.** Shape into 4 rectangles, and chill.
2. Pound **chicken breasts** with a meat mallet until ¼-inch thick. Place a rectangle of butter in the center of each, turn in the ends, and roll up tightly to enclose the butter. Secure with toothpicks.
3. Roll in **Seasoned Flour.** Dip in the **egg-and-water** mixture, then in **bread crumbs.** Chill for about 2 hours.
4. Deep fry chicken in **oil** at 375°F for 7 minutes. Place on absorbent paper to drain.

Chicken Lasagna

This chicken pasta dish is rich in carbohydrates and low in fat. It goes well with a tossed green salad and garlic bread.

Servings 4 to 6

Total Time ⌛ ⌛

Major Utensils Large saucepan
Large, deep skillet
Lasagna pan

Ingredients
1 small chicken, boned and minced
½ pound lasagna
1 onion, chopped
½ cup oil
3 tablespoons butter
2 cloves of garlic, crushed
4 slices of bacon, diced
1 cup dry wine, red or white
1½ pounds fresh tomatoes, peeled and seeded, or
   2 large cans Italian (plum) tomatoes
Salt and pepper
Parmesan cheese, grated
Parsley, chopped

Step by Step

1. In a large saucepan, boil **lasagna** in salted water until just tender 10–15 minutes. Drain, rinse with boiling water, and drain again. Set aside.

2. Meanwhile, sauté **onion** lightly in **oil** and **butter** in a skillet over medium heat until transparent.

3. Add **garlic, bacon,** and **chicken**, and cook until chicken is golden.

4. Stir in **wine** and **tomatoes**; season to taste with **salt and pepper**. Simmer for 30–40 minutes.

5. In lasagna pan, alternate layers of cooked noodles and sauce, beginning and ending with sauce. Sprinkle with **Parmesan cheese** and **parsley**.

6. Bake at 400°F until top is golden and lasagna bubbles (about 15–20 minutes).

Instead of using meat from a small chicken, grind the dark meat from a large bird, saving the breasts for another recipe.

Chicken Leg Ring

This dish provides a satisfying meal at a reasonably low price. For optimum nutritional value, include another vegetable.

Servings	4
Total Time	⏳
Major Utensil	Shallow casserole
Ingredients	**8 chicken drumsticks** **Salt and pepper** **Vegetable oil** **Mashed Potatoes (below)** **Parsley, chopped**
Step by Step	**1.** Season **chicken drumsticks** with **salt and pepper,** and brush with **oil.** In casserole, bake at 400°F until chicken is tender (about 1 hour), basting frequently with pan juices. **2.** About 30 minutes after putting chicken in oven, prepare **Mashed Potatoes**. Keep warm until chicken is cooked. **3.** Pile potatoes in the center of a serving platter and arrange chicken legs in a ring around them. **4.** Garnish with **parsley** before serving.

Mashed Potatoes

Boil **4 medium, peeled potatoes** until soft (about 15 minutes). Drain well; return to pan and dry over low heat. Add **3 tablespoons butter, 1 teaspoon salt**, and **⅓ cup hot milk**. Mash with a fork, eggbeater, or potato masher; or put through a potato ricer or sieve. Place pan in a bowl of hot water to keep warm. Old potatoes are preferable to new for mashing. To hasten cooking, cut potatoes in pieces.

Chicken Legs Chaud-Froid

The chaud-froid *sauce called for in this recipe is indeed versatile. In different forms, it is used to enhance a variety of egg, meat, fish, and shellfish dishes. Often, it is flavored with Madeira or sherry. In Sicily, pistachio nuts are added.*

Servings   4

Total Time   ⏳ ⏳ ⏳

Major Utensils   Small skillet
Trussing needle and string
Roasting pan
Double boiler

Ingredients   4 chicken legs, boned (see Step 3, page 20)
½ onion, chopped
1-2 cloves of garlic, crushed
½ pound ground pork
½ pound ground veal
1 egg
1 tablespoon parsley, chopped
Salt and pepper
Melted butter or fat

Chaud-froid Sauce   6 tablespoons butter
6 tablespoons flour
2 cups milk
1 tablespoon gelatin, softened in 2 tablespoons cold water

Garnish   **Stuffed olives, sliced**
Black olives, pitted and sliced
Parsley, chopped

Glaze   **2 cups Clarified Jellied Consommé**
(see page 10)

Step by Step   **1.** In a small skillet, sauté **onion** lightly. Combine with **garlic, pork, veal, egg,** and **parsley.** Season lightly with **salt and pepper.**
2. Cut a slit in each **chicken leg,** and stuff with the pork-and-veal mixture. With string, truss the legs.
3. Brush with **butter or fat,** and place in a greased roasting pan. Roast at 350°F for about 1 hour.
4. Remove chicken legs from the oven and set aside to cool.
5. When cool, carefully skin the cooked chicken legs, and place them on a wire rack.
6. Make the Chaud-froid Sauce by melting **butter** in the top of a double boiler until it is transparent. Add **flour** all at once. Cook mixture directly over medium heat, stirring constantly until it becomes frothy.

Step by Step Continued

- Return to double boiler. Pour in **milk**; stir with a whisk until sauce thickens.
- Gradually stir in gelatin.

7. Pour Chaud-froid Sauce over the chicken legs. Allow 15 minutes for sauce to set.

8. Garnish coated chicken legs with **stuffed olives, black olives,** and **parsley.** Allow the garnish to set.

9. Glaze garnished chicken legs with **Clarified Jellied Consommé**.

Almond Dressing

Chop finely **1 pound mushrooms, 1 small green pepper, 1 small onion, 1 stalk of celery,** and **chicken giblets**. Place in a large skillet, and sauté over medium–low heat in **2 tablespoons oil** and **2 tablespoons butter,** along with **2 tablespoons parsley,** for 5 minutes. Soak **1 cup bread cubes** in **chicken broth** until soft. Stir into mushroom mixture. Add **1 cup slivered almonds**. Season to taste with **salt, pepper,** and **Poultry Seasoning** (see page 134). Cook for a few minutes over low heat. Transfer dressing to a greased casserole; bake for 1 hour alongside chicken.

Chicken Log

Chicken spread and round white bread slices form this attractive loaf. Coated with nuts or chopped parsley, it is impressive on a buffet table. Radish roses, carrots, and green and red peppers are colorful additions to the serving platter.

Servings	8
Total Time	⏳ ⏳ ⏳
Major Utensils	Large, flat serving platter Pastry bag
Ingredients	**4 cups cooked chicken, ground 1 cup butter ½ cup Mayonnaise (below) 3 cloves of garlic, crushed ½ cup celery, chopped Thyme Marjoram Parsley Salt and pepper 1 round loaf white bread, sliced**
Coating	**1 pound cream cheese or butter, softened ½ cup ground walnuts or finely chopped parsley**
Garnish	**Cream cheese, softened**
Step by Step	1. Blend the **ground chicken** with the **butter, Mayonnaise, garlic**, and **celery**, along with **thyme, marjoram, parsley, salt**, and **pepper**, to taste. 2. Spread this mixture on both sides of each slice of **bread**. 3. On the serving platter, reassemble the loaf to form a log. Cover and refrigerate for several hours. 4. Spread **cream cheese or butter** on the log then roll in **walnuts or parsley**. 5. Decorate with **cream cheese** piping applied with a pastry bag.

🍲🍲🍲 Mayonnaise

Place in a blender **¼ cup vegetable oil**, **1 egg**, **2 tablespoons vinegar**, **¾ teaspoon salt**, **½ teaspoon dry mustard**, and **¼ teaspoon paprika**. Slowly pour **¾ cup vegetable oil** into blender while processing the ingredients at *Low*.

Chicken Madrid

Flavor in this Spanish-style dish is accented by the use of turmeric, a member of the ginger family. Turmeric appears in many forms, but the light-colored Madras variety is generally considered the best.

Servings 4 to 6

Total Time ⧖ ⧖

Major Utensil Large, deep ovenproof skillet

Ingredients
- 1 small chicken, skinned and cut in pieces (see pages 4 and 5)
- 3 tablespoons flour
- Salt and pepper
- 2 tablespoons butter
- 2 tablespoons oil
- 2 medium onions, sliced
- 2 cloves of garlic, minced
- 1 green pepper, chopped
- ½ cup pimentos
- 1 cup rice
- 1 teaspoon turmeric
- 3 cups Chicken Stock (see page 10)

Step by Step

1. Coat **chicken** pieces lightly with **flour, salt,** and **pepper.** Sauté in skillet in **butter and oil** over medium heat until browned. Remove from skillet and set aside.

2. In the same pan, sauté **onion, garlic,** and **green pepper** until onion is golden. Add **pimento** and **rice**; cook for 2 minutes, stirring.

3. Add **turmeric** and **Chicken Stock**; stir, and bring to boil.

4. Remove from heat, and return chicken to the pan.

5. Cover lightly with aluminum foil, but do not seal the edges. Bake in a 350°F oven until chicken is tender (about 90 minutes).

Chicken Maryland

Fried bananas and broiled bacon rolls add an original touch to this well-known fried-chicken dish. The corn fritters, however, are traditional.

Servings	6
Total Time	⏳ ⏳
Major Utensils	2 large skillets, one with cover Blender 2 skewers
Ingredients	**1 small chicken, skinned and cut in pieces (see page 4)** **Seasoned Flour (see page 28)** **1 egg, beaten lightly** **1½ –2 cups fresh white bread crumbs** **8–10 tablespoons unsalted butter** **8 lean bacon slices, cut in half and rolled** **3 bananas, peeled and cut in half**
Corn Fritters	**2 tablespoons flour** **2 eggs, beaten lightly** **2 cups whole kernel corn** **1 teaspoon salt** **¼ teaspoon pepper** **1 tablespoon olive or corn oil**
Garnish	**Watercress**
Step by Step	**1.** Coat the **skinned chicken pieces** with **Seasoned Flour,** dip in the **egg,** and coat with **bread crumbs.** Shake off any loose crumbs. **2.** Melt about **4 tablespoons of the butter** in a large skillet and sauté the chicken until brown on both sides (about 10 minutes). Turn down the heat, cover the pan, and cook gently, turning the chicken once, for 25–30 minutes. **3.** While the chicken cooks, thread the **bacon rolls** on two skewers. Coat **bananas** with Seasoned Flour. Set aside. **4.** To make the corn fritter batter, put the **flour, eggs, corn, salt,** and **pepper** in a blender and whirl until thoroughly mixed. Set aside. **5.** When the chicken pieces are tender, transfer them to a serving dish and keep them warm. **6.** Melt **2 tablespoons of butter** in the skillet, add the bananas, and sauté them over low heat. **7.** At the same time, heat the **remaining butter** and the **oil** in a second skillet. When hot, add tablespoons of the corn fritter batter and cook until golden brown on each side. **8.** While the last fritters are cooking, put the skewers with bacon rolls under a hot broiler for about 2 minutes. **9.** Serve the chicken pieces along with the corn fritters, bacon rolls, and fried bananas. Garnish with sprigs of **watercress.**

This recipe is illustrated on page 35.

Chicken Pie with Cheese Pastry

The delicious crust used in this recipe is usually best when made from sharp or very sharp cheese. Cheddar is a good choice.

Servings   6 to 8

Total Time   ⏳ ⏳ ⏳

Major Utensils   Stockpot, with cover
Medium saucepan
Pie dish or shallow casserole

Ingredients
1 large chicken
2 onions
2 carrots
4 stalks of celery
Salt and pepper
5 tablespoons butter
5 tablespoons flour
1 cup milk
Cheese Pastry (below)

Step by Step

1. Place **chicken** in a stockpot with **onions, carrots, celery, salt and pepper.** Cover with water. Place cover on pan and bring to boil; reduce heat, and simmer until chicken is tender (about 1 hour).

2. Cool. Strain broth.

3. Prepare sauce by melting **butter** in saucepan. Blend in **flour,** and cook briefly, stirring. Add **milk** and 1 cup of the strained chicken broth; simmer for a few minutes, stirring constantly. Add salt and pepper to taste. Set aside to cool.

4. Bone chicken, cut in pieces, and place in a shallow casserole or pie dish.

5. Dice onions, carrots, and celery. Stir into chicken, along with sauce. Cover with **Cheese Pastry.**

6. Bake at 375°F until pastry is golden, about 45 minutes. (The unbaked pie can be frozen; bake without thawing at 375°F for about 1 hour 30 minutes.)

🍲🍲🍲 Cheese Pastry

Measure **2 cups flour** without sifting. Add **2 tablespoons baking powder, 1 teaspoon salt,** and **½ cup grated cheese.** Toss with a fork to blend. Cut in **¼ cup butter** or **shortening** with two knives, or rub in gently with fingertips. Beat **1 egg** in **¾ cup milk.** Make a well in the flour mixture, add the liquid, and stir gently until mixture forms a ball. If time allows, chill before rolling out.

Chicken Poached with Potatoes

This is a classic French recipe known as Bonne Femme. Apart from the potatoes, many other fresh vegetables can be added.

Servings 4

Total Time ⏳ ⏳

Major Utensil Large, deep skillet with cover

Ingredients
- **1 small chicken, cut in pieces (see page 4)**
- **2 tablespoons flour**
- **1 teaspoon salt**
- **¼ teaspoon pepper**
- **¼ teaspoon thyme or curry powder**
- **⅓ cup butter, chicken fat or vegetable oil**
- **2 cloves of garlic or 1 onion, minced**
- **8 to 10 small potatoes, peeled**
- **2 cups Chicken Stock (see page 10) or water**

Step by Step

1. Combine **flour, salt, pepper**, and **thyme** or **curry powder** in a paper bag.

2. Put **chicken pieces**, individually, into bag and shake until lightly coated.

3. In a skillet, add chicken and **garlic** or **onion** to **butter, chicken fat**, or **oil**. Brown meat on all sides, drain on paper towels, then return to the pan.

4. Add potatoes; pour in **Chicken Stock** or **water**. Cover tightly, and poach over low heat until chicken is tender (40–50 minutes).

5. Remove chicken and potatoes; place on a serving platter and keep warm.

6. Boil liquid over high heat until slightly reduced. Pour over chicken before serving.

Substitute duck or goose for chicken. The meat will be less fatty than if the birds were roasted. Degrease sauce, however, before reducing it.

Chicken Provence Style

The term Provence style (in French, Provençale*) refers to two ingredients—tomatoes and garlic—that are typical of dishes prepared in the Provence region of southeastern France.*

Servings 4 to 6

Total Time ⏳ ⏳

Major Utensils Flameproof casserole with cover
Large skillet

Ingredients
- **2 small chickens, cut in pieces (see page 4)**
- **4 tablespoons butter or 2 tablespoons butter and 2 tablespoons oil**
- **½ cup white wine**
- **1 clove of garlic, crushed**
- **1 cup Tomato Brown Sauce (see page 11)**
- **½ cup vegetable oil**
- **3 onions, chopped**
- **2 eggplants, sliced, salted, and dried**
- **4 tomatoes, coarsely chopped**

Step by Step

1. In the casserole, sauté **chicken pieces** in hot **butter,** or **butter and oil,** over medium heat until brown. Cover and bake at 325°F until chicken is tender (about 45 minutes). Remove chicken and keep hot.

2. Add **wine** to the casserole; scrape pan and mix with pan juices. Add **garlic** and simmer gently until liquid is reduced by half.

3. Add **Tomato Brown Sauce** and chicken pieces; simmer 3–4 minutes.

4. In a large skillet, sauté the **onions** in **oil** over medium heat until light brown, then set aside.

5. In the same pan, brown the **eggplant slices** on both sides, adding oil as necessary. Remove from pan and set aside.

6. Add **tomatoes** to the pan and sauté gently 1–2 minutes.

7. Add onions, eggplant, and tomatoes to the chicken and heat through.

To prevent eggplant from discoloring, sprinkle slices with lemon juice. Because this vegetable is excessively moist, it is important to salt, then dry slices before cooking them. Be sure to brown them in hot oil; eggplant asborbs great quantities of oil that is not well heated.

Chicken Saint Sylvester

Sautéed chicken breasts and red wine sauce combine simply and easily in this classic French recipe. Fit for any special occasion, it is traditional New Year's fare in France, where it is named Suprême de Volaille Saint-Sylvestre, *after the saint whose feast day falls on December 31.*

Servings   4

Total Time   ⌛

Major Utensil   Large skillet

Ingredients   4 chicken breasts, boned (see page 5)
10 tablespoons unsalted butter
1 shallot, finely chopped
½ cup red wine
½ cup Chicken Stock (see page 10)
Salt and pepper

Step by Step
1. Cook the **chicken** in **4 tablespoons** of the **butter** over gentle heat for 25 minutes, or until tender. Arrange on a serving dish.
2. Add the **shallot** to the pan, with the **wine.** Bring to boil and continue boiling for 1 minute.
3. Add the **Chicken Stock** and boil briskly until reduced by half.
4. Stir in the **remaining butter,** in small knobs, and season with **salt** and **pepper,** to taste. To serve, pour the sauce over the chicken.

●●● Butter Spread

Beat **1 cup vegetable oil** into **1 pound of butter.** The resulting spread retains the taste of butter, while being lower in saturated fats. This mixture is also easier to handle cold than butter because it is softer. It can be used in any recipe that calls for butter.

This recipe is illustrated on page 53.

Chicken Salad

The secret of a good chicken salad is to dice the meat in large chunks. If the pieces are too small, the chicken will not be as tasty. Belgian endives lend a distinctive flavor to this classic luncheon dish.

Servings	6
Total Time	⏳
Major Utensil	Large bowl
Ingredients	3 cups poached chicken (see page 7), diced 1 orange, peeled and sectioned 1 slice Bermuda onion, minced ¼ cup pitted black olives, sliced ½ cup French Dressing (below) ½ cup Mayonnaise (see page 42) Salt and pepper 3 Belgian endives
Step by Step	**1.** Chop each **orange section** into 3 pieces. Place, with juice, in a bowl. **2.** Add **chicken, Bermuda onion,** and **olives.** Toss to mix. **3.** Blend in **French Dressing** and **Mayonnaise.** Season to taste with **salt** and **pepper.** **4.** Serve on **endive** leaves arranged like wheel spokes.

🍲🍲🍲 French Dressing

Combine the following ingredients in a blender, glass jar, or small mixing bowl: **2 tablespoons fresh lemon juice, 2 tablespoons cider vinegar, ¾ cup salad oil, 1 teaspoon salt, ¼ teaspoon pepper, 1 teaspoon Worcestershire sauce, ½ teaspoon paprika, ¼ teaspoon garlic powder, and ½ teaspoon sugar.** Blend, shake, or beat with a rotary beater. Shake hard before using.

Chicken Sauté with Madeira

Madeira is a fortified, white to amber dessert wine. Used in this recipe, with cognac, it turns an ordinary white sauce into something special. Steamed asparagus goes well with this dish.

Servings	4 to 6
Total Time	⏳
Major Utensils	Large, ovenproof skillet with cover Double boiler
Ingredients	**1 small chicken, skinned and cut in pieces (see page 4)** **4 tablespoons butter or 2 tablespoons butter and 2 tablespoons oil** **Salt and pepper** **½ cup Madeira** **¼ cup cognac** **½ cup light cream**
White Sauce	**2 tablespoons butter** **2 tablespoons flour** **1 cup milk** **Salt and pepper**
Step by Step	**1.** Season the **chicken pieces** with **salt and pepper.** Sauté over medium heat in **butter** or **butter and oil** until golden brown. **2.** Cover the skillet and place in a moderately hot oven (325°F). Cook chicken until tender (about 25 minutes). Remove from pan and set aside. **3.** Add **Madeira** and **cognac** to the skillet and scrape the pan to dissolve any lumps. Bring liquid to boil and reduce by half. **4.** Meanwhile, prepare White Sauce by melting the **butter** in a double boiler. When butter is transparent, add the **flour.** Place the pan directly on the burner and stir briskly over medium heat until the mixture is frothy. Return to the double boiler, slowly pour in the **milk,** and cook, stirring continuously, until the sauce thickens. Season to taste with **salt and pepper.** **5.** Add White Sauce and **cream** to the chicken liquid. Stir thoroughly, then return the chicken to the pan. Simmer for a few minutes. **6.** Arrange the chicken on a serving platter and cover with sauce.

When you cook poultry in liquid, add a dash of baking soda. Combined with the liquid, it makes an effective, easy-to-obtain tenderizer.

Chicken Stew with Okra

This is a simple and mild version of a Creole gumbo, not authentic but delicious, and easy to prepare. To give it more of the flavor of Louisiana-style cooking, add hot-pepper sauce. Serve over rice in deep plates.

Servings 6 to 8

Total Time ⏳ ⏳

Major Utensil Large, deep skillet with cover

Ingredients
1 medium chicken, chopped in small chunks (see page 4)
¼ cup peanut oil or corn oil
2 large onions, chopped
2 green peppers, sliced
1 tablespoon sugar
2 teaspoons salt
4 cups Stewed Tomatoes (below)
1 pound small okra, whole or sliced as preferred
Chicken Stock (see page 10) or water

Step by Step
1. In the skillet, brown **chicken pieces** in **oil**; remove and set aside.
2. In the same pan, sauté **onions** and **green peppers** until lightly browned. Pour off fat. Sprinkle vegetables with **sugar**.
3. Return chicken to pan, and sprinkle with **salt**. Add **Stewed Tomatoes**. Cover; simmer until chicken is cooked (about 40 minutes).
4. Add **okra** (sliced okra helps thicken the stew), and simmer for 10 minutes. Add a little **Chicken Stock** or **water** if tomatoes cook away too quickly. Stew is juicy when done.

Stewed Tomatoes

Simmer **1 large can of tomatoes** for about 10 minutes with ¾ teaspoon salt, ¼ teaspoon paprika, 2 teaspoons sugar, ½ teaspoon basil, and 1 tablespoon butter. Makes approximately 2 cups.

Chicken Tetrazzini

This famous Italian dish was named after an equally illustrious Italian operatic soprano, Luisa Tetrazzini (1871–1940). It is served with pasta—usually noodles or macaroni.

Servings 4

Total Time ⧖ ⧖

Major Utensils Deep skillet
Large pot with cover

Ingredients
1 small chicken, cut in pieces (see page 4)
2 tablespoons oil
2 tablespoons butter
8 large mushrooms, thinly sliced
1 medium onion, sliced
¼ cup white wine
¼ cup brandy
2 tablespoons parsley, chopped
¾ cup heavy cream
2 tablespoons flour
3 tablespoons soft butter
Salt and pepper

Side dish Macaroni or noodles

Garnish Parmesan cheese, grated

Step by Step
1. Place **chicken pieces** in skillet and cover with water. Cook gently, covered, until meat is tender (about 40 minutes). Remove chicken; bone, skin, and slice into large chunks. Strain broth; reserve.
2. In a pot, cook **noodles** or **macaroni** according to package instructions.
3. Meanwhile, heat **oil** and **butter** in the skillet and sauté the chicken for a few minutes, until golden. Add **mushrooms** and **onion** and sauté a few minutes more.
4. Stir in **wine, brandy,** ¾ cup of the strained broth, **parsley,** and **cream.** Simmer for 5 minutes.
5. In a small cup, mix the **butter** and **flour** into a paste. Add to the skillet slowly, stirring constantly, and cook until the sauce thickens slightly. Season to taste with **salt and pepper.**
6. Serve over macaroni or noodles. Sprinkle with **Parmesan cheese.**

Chicken Saint Sylvester (see page 48).▲
Gardener's Chicken (see page 77).▶

Chicken Torcello

This is a specialty of Torcello, an island near Venice. It is an elegant pasta dish, yet nonetheless quick to prepare.

Servings 4

Total Time ⏳

Major Utensils Large skillet with cover
Large pot

Ingredients
1 small chicken, cut in pieces (see page 4)
2 tablespoons flour
½ teaspoon salt
1 teaspoon paprika
1 teaspoon basil
½ teaspoon garlic powder
2 tablespoons olive oil
1 tablespoon butter
1 cup Chicken Stock (see page 10)
4 large tomatoes, peeled, seeded, and coarsely chopped
½ cup parsley, minced
1 green pepper, diced
8 ounces thin spaghetti
½ cup Parmesan cheese, grated

Step by Step

1. On a plate, season the **flour** with **salt, paprika, basil**, and **garlic powder**.
2. Roll **chicken pieces** in this mixture.
3. In a skillet, brown chicken pieces in **olive oil** and **butter**. Add **Chicken Stock** and **tomatoes**. Bring to boil, cover, and simmer until chicken is tender (about 30 minutes).
4. Uncover, and boil to reduce liquid to the consistency of light cream.
5. Add **parsley** and **green pepper**. Cover, remove from heat; set aside in a warm place.
6. Meanwhile, prepare **spaghetti** in a pot according to directions on package. Place on a serving platter and pour chicken and sauce on top. Sprinkle with **Parmesan cheese** before serving.

Chicken Vienna

Leave the dinner in the oven to cook while you tend to your guests; you'll need only a few minutes at the end to thicken the sauce. For a final flourish, garnish the chicken with cucumber cut in chunks and simmered in butter.

Servings   4 to 5

Total Time   ⏳ ⏳

Major Utensil   Large, deep skillet with cover

Ingredients
1 medium chicken, cut in pieces (see page 4)
Salt and pepper
1 onion, finely chopped
2 tablespoons butter
1 green pepper, chopped
2 carrots, sliced
6 mushrooms, thinly sliced
1 fresh tomato or ¼ cup canned tomatoes
1 teaspoon paprika
1–2 cups water
Beurre Manié (below)
¼ cup heavy cream

Step by Step
1. Season **chicken pieces** with **salt and pepper.** Sauté **onion** lightly in **butter** over medium heat; add seasoned chicken and sauté until browned.
2. Add **green pepper, carrots, mushrooms, tomato, paprika,** salt, and pepper. Add 1–2 cups **water**, or more, as needed. Cover and cook gently until chicken is tender (about 45 minutes).
3. Adjust seasoning. Thicken pan juices with **Beurre Manié.** Stir in **cream** and simmer for a few minutes.

Beurre Manié

Knead **2 tablespoons butter** and **4 tablespoons flour** into a paste. Add small pieces of this paste to a hot liquid that needs thickening.

Chicken Wings with Mushrooms

These tangy wings with mushrooms and rice provide sumptuous fare at budget price.

Servings	4 to 6
Total Time	⏳ ⏳
Major Utensils	Broiling pan Small saucepan
Ingredients	**24 chicken wings** **¼ cup soy sauce** **4 green onions or 1 small onion, finely chopped** **¼ cup sherry** **Sugar** **½ cup Chicken Stock (see page 10)** **2 tablespoons cornstarch** **2 cans mushrooms, drained**
Side dish	**Rice Pilaf (see page 61)**
Step by Step	**1.** Marinate **chicken wings** in **soy sauce** for 30 minutes. Drain chicken, reserving sauce. Place on a greased broiling pan, and bake in 350°F oven for 1 hour, frequently turning and basting with pan juices. **2.** Meanwhile, prepare **Rice Pilaf**. **3.** About 10 minutes before chicken is ready, prepare sauce by mixing in a saucepan **green onions** or **onion, sherry,** a pinch of **sugar, Chicken Stock,** and **cornstarch** with reserved soy sauce; heat until transparent and add **mushrooms**. **4.** Arrange chicken wings on a serving platter and pour sauce over them. Serve with **Rice Pilaf**.

 Instead of canned mushrooms, use 1 pound fresh mushrooms, thinly sliced and lightly sautéed in 2 tablespoons butter and 2 tablespoons oil.

Chicken with Garlic

Don't let 40 cloves of garlic frighten you. Like onion, garlic becomes mellow and sweet when cooked.

Servings	4 to 6
Total Time	⏳ ⏳ ⏳
Major Utensil	Large, deep casserole with cover
Ingredients	**1 large chicken** **½ cup olive oil** **1 Bouquet Garni (see page 110)** **40 cloves of garlic, peeled** **1 bay leaf** **2 sprigs of parsley, coarsely chopped** **2 stalks of celery, chopped** **Rosemary** **Thyme** **Sage** **Salt and pepper**
Seal	**2 cups flour** **1 cup cold water**
Garnish	**Garlic Croutons (below)**
Step by Step	**1.** Brush **chicken** with **olive oil,** and put **Bouquet Garni** into the cavity. **2.** Place chicken in a casserole, and surround with **garlic cloves, bay leaf, parsley, celery,** a pinch each of **rosemary, thyme, sage,** and **salt and pepper.** Cover. **3.** Make a thick paste of **flour** and **water,** and press around edge of cover to seal casserole. Bake in a 350°F oven for approximately 2 hours 30 minutes, calculating 20 minutes per pound of chicken. **4.** Garnish with **Garlic Croutons** before serving.

Garlic Croutons

Cook **1 clove of garlic** in **½ cup vegetable oil** over medium heat until garlic is golden. Discard garlic. Add **bread cubes** cut from 3 slices of bread. Cook until cubes are golden. Drain.

Chicken with Mushrooms

The subtle blend of mushrooms, white wine, and lemon juice adds distinctive flavor to sautéed chicken. If brown sauce is on hand, preparation time for this recipe is about 15 minutes.

Servings 4 to 6

Total Time ⏳ ⏳

Major Utensils Ovenproof skillet with cover
Medium skillet

Ingredients **2 small chickens, cut in pieces (see page 4)**
½ cup butter or ¼ cup butter and
 ¼ cup oil
4 green onions, finely chopped
½ cup white wine
2 tablespoons Brown Sauce (see page 11)
¼ pound mushrooms, thinly sliced
Lemon juice

Garnish **Parsley, chopped**

Step by Step **1.** In a skillet, sauté **chicken pieces** in ¼ **cup butter,** or **butter and oil,** over medium heat until brown. Cover and bake at 325°F until chicken is tender (about 45 minutes). Transfer to serving platter and keep hot.
2. Sauté **green onions** lightly in the skillet. Add **white wine** and stir to blend with pan juices; boil the liquid to reduce by half.
3. Add **Brown Sauce** and **a few drops of lemon juice.**
4. In a second skillet, sauté **mushrooms** in **remaining butter** or **butter and oil** until cooked, but not brown, and add to sauce. Cook over low heat for 5 minutes and pour over chicken. Garnish with **parsley.**

Chicken with Orange and Onion

Small chicken breasts are best suited for this tangy dish. Serve with rice and a tossed green salad for a simple, delicious meal.

Servings	6
Total Time	⌛
Major Utensil	Large skillet
Ingredients	**6 chicken breasts, boned if preferred** **6 tablespoons peanut oil** **2 tablespoons butter** **12 orange slices** **1 large red onion, cut in 6 slices** **½ cup Chicken Stock (see page 10)** **Pepper**
Garnish	**Watercress**
Step by Step	**1.** In the skillet, brown **chicken breasts** in **oil** and **butter** until golden and tender (about 12 minutes with bones, 8 minutes without). Transfer to a serving plate and keep warm. **2.** Sauté **orange slices** in the pan juices until lightly browned. Remove from pan and set aside. **3.** Sauté **onion slices** for about 4 minutes in the same skillet, adding more butter and oil if necessary. Remove from pan and set aside. **4.** Pour **Chicken Stock** into skillet and cook over high heat, scraping pan bottom, until liquid is reduced to about 6 tablespoons. **5.** Place 2 orange slices on each chicken breast, crown with 1 onion slice each. Pour a spoonful of sauce over each breast. Sprinkle with pepper and garnish with **watercress** before serving.

Chicken with Rice Pilaf

A creamy sauce dresses up this version of a hearty "boiled dinner." The broth from the chicken and vegetables gives a deliciously rich flavor to the Supreme Sauce.

Servings	6
Total Time	⏳ ⏳
Major Utensils	Stockpot with cover Flameproof casserole with cover
Ingredients	**1 medium chicken** **4 carrots** **2 leeks, white part only** **2 onions** **Salt and peppercorns** **2 whole cloves** **Bouquet Garni (see page 110)** **2 cups Supreme Sauce (see page 11)**
Side Dish	**Rice Pilaf**
Step by Step	**1.** Place **chicken** in stockpot. Cover with water, bring to boil, and continue boiling for 3–4 minutes. **2.** Lower heat. Add **carrots, leeks, onions, salt, peppercorns, cloves**, and the **Bouquet Garni**. Cover, and simmer until chicken and vegetables are tender (about 1 hour 30 minutes). **3.** Meanwhile, prepare **Rice Pilaf**. **4.** Remove chicken and vegetables, and place in middle of serving platter; keep warm. Strain broth. **5.** Prepare **Supreme Sauce** using strained broth. **6.** Surround chicken with Rice Pilaf. Pour Supreme Sauce over it, or serve separately.

🍲🍲🍲 Rice Pilaf

In a flameproof casserole, sauté **1 chopped onion** lightly in **4 tablespoons butter** until transparent, but not brown. Add **1 cup long-grain rice**, and cook for a few minutes longer, stirring. Stir in **2 cups Chicken Stock (see page 10), 1 clove of garlic, 1 bay leaf, 2 cloves,** and **salt** and **pepper**, to taste. Bring to boil, then cover and place in a 350°F oven for 20 minutes. If all the liquid has not been absorbed after 20 minutes, return to the oven without stirring, and cook further. Remove cloves, garlic, and bay leaf before serving.

Chicken with Sautéed Vegetables

Any dish that uses fresh vegetables tastes better—and is more nutritious—than one based on preserved produce. In this recipe, the vegetables are mainly root kinds—carrots, turnips, and potatoes—which are sold fresh year-round.

Servings	4 to 6
Total Time	⧖ ⧖
Major Utensils	Ovenproof skillet with cover Large skillet
Ingredients	**2 small chickens, cut in pieces (see page 4)** **½ cup butter** **¼ pound Blanched Salt Pork, diced (see page 21)** **6 medium carrots, sliced** **1 small turnip, sliced** **4 medium potatoes, sliced** **½ pound green beans, trimmed** **½ cup white wine** **1 cup Brown Sauce (see page 11)** **Salt and pepper**
Step by Step	**1.** In the ovenproof skillet, sauté **chicken pieces** in **¼ cup butter** over medium heat until brown. Cover and bake at 325°F until chicken is tender (about 45 minutes). **2.** While the chicken is cooking, fry the **Blanched Salt Pork** in large skillet until golden. Add the **carrots, turnips, potatoes**, and **green beans** with **¼ cup butter** and sauté until tender. **3.** When chicken is cooked, remove from the skillet and add **white wine** and **salt and pepper** to taste, to the pan. Scrape the bottom with a spoon to mix in chicken bits thoroughly; boil the liquid to reduce by half. **4.** Add the **Brown Sauce** and cook for a few minutes. Return the chicken to the pan and warm it up. **5.** Serve the chicken on a platter. Arrange the vegetables alongside. The gravy is served separately.

Chicken with Sour Cream

A touch of Parmesan, combined with currant jelly, brings a highly original flavor to this recipe for four. Parmesan is a hard cheese made from skim milk and fermented over a period of 4 years. Once ripe, it should be golden yellow and should sweat slightly.

Servings 4

Total Time ⌛

Major Utensils Deep skillet
Ovenproof platter

Ingredients
4 chicken breasts, boned (see page 5)
3 tablespoons flour
4 tablespoons butter
3 tablespoons sherry
1 teaspoon catsup or Sugarless Catsup (see page 66)
½ cup Chicken Stock (see page 10)
1½ cups sour cream
1 tablespoon currant jelly
3 tablespoons Parmesan cheese, grated
Salt and pepper
2 cups mushrooms, sliced
Cayenne pepper
1 tablespoon dillweed

Step by Step

1. Dust **chicken** with **2 tablespoons flour**; brown in **2 tablespoons butter** in deep skillet over medium heat. Remove from heat. Pour **2 tablespoons sherry** over chicken; stir well. Remove chicken from pan and set aside.

2. Add **catsup** and **remaining flour** to the pan, stirring to make a smooth paste. Pour in **Chicken Stock**. Stir and cook slowly until mixture thickens.

3. Slowly add **sour cream**. Blend in **currant jelly, 1 tablespoon Parmesan cheese**, and **salt** and **pepper**, to taste. Return chicken to pan and cook gently until tender (about 20 minutes).

4. Remove chicken and place it on an ovenproof platter. Pour sauce over it, sprinkle with **remaining Parmesan cheese**. Broil until brown.

5. Meanwhile, sauté **mushrooms** in **remaining butter** with a dash of **cayenne pepper**. Season with **remaining** sherry. Add **dillweed**. Pour over browned chicken before serving.

Chicken with Truffles

The most highly esteemed members of the truffle family come from the regions of Périgord and the Lot river in France. If this delicacy is unavailable, substitute black olives. For an authentic accent, use a variety cultivated in France especially for the table, the picholine.

Servings	5 to 6
Total Time	⏳ ⏳
Major Utensils	Large saucepan Flameproof casserole with cover
Ingredients	**1 veal shank, cut in two 1 medium chicken 6 slices of truffle or black olives 1 cup sliced carrots 1 cup sliced leek, white part only Salt and pepper**
Seal	**2 cups flour 1 cup cold water**
Garnish	**Pickles or pickled cherries**
Step by Step	**1.** In a saucepan, cover **veal shank** with water and cook for 30 minutes. Season with **salt** and **pepper**. Set veal aside in its broth to cool. **2.** Insert slices of **truffle** or **black olive** between the skin and breast meat of the **chicken**. Truss the chicken (see page 5) and place it in a casserole just big enough to hold it. Add **carrots** and **leek**. **3.** Bone the veal shank, and add it to the casserole along with its broth. Add water, if necessary, to cover all ingredients. Season to taste with salt and pepper. Cover and bring slowly to a boil. **4.** Make a paste with the **flour** and **water,** and use it to seal the cover. **5.** Bake at 350°F for about 1 hour. **6.** Let stand for 15 minutes before removing cover. Discard paste seal. Serve chicken with the vegetables and broth, garnished with **pickles** or **pickled cherries.**

Chinese Chicken Casserole

This sumptuous luncheon dish can be prepared in advance and stored in the freezer until needed.

Servings   6

Total Time   ⏳ ⏳

Major Utensils   Deep skillet with cover
Large saucepan
Baking dish

Ingredients
1 medium chicken, cut in pieces
1 onion, quartered
2 celery stalks with tops
½ pound green noodles
4-6 carrots, sliced
6 tablespoons butter
4 tablespoons flour
2 tablespoons heavy cream
Salt and pepper
8 canned water chestnuts, sliced
½ cup soft bread cubes

Step by Step

1. Place **chicken pieces, onion,** and **celery** in a deep skillet; cover with water. Cover, and simmer until chicken is tender (about 45 minutes). Remove chicken from broth to cool. Strain broth and reserve 2 cups for use in sauce.

2. Meanwhile, boil **noodles** in a large saucepan for 6 minutes in salted water. Drain. Place in buttered baking dish.

3. In the same pan, steam-cook **carrots** until tender (about 6 minutes). Set aside.

4. Melt **4 tablespoons butter** in the skillet; add **flour**. Blend in reserved broth and **cream**. Stir constantly until thickened. Season to taste with **salt and pepper**. Add chicken pieces, carrots, and **water chestnuts**, and pour over noodles.

5. Sauté **bread cubes** in **remaining butter** until golden. Sprinkle over chicken. Bake at 375°F until hot and bubbling (about 30 minutes).

Chinese Deviled Chicken

The Chinese part of this recipe is the blanching performed before broiling. Chicken breasts can be substituted for the chicken pieces.

Servings 4

Total Time ⏳

Major Utensils Broiling pan
Small saucepan

Ingredients 1 small chicken, cut in pieces (see page 4)
4 tablespoons butter or peanut oil
1 tablespoon cider or wine vinegar
½ teaspoon tarragon
1 teaspoon dry mustard
1 teaspoon sugar
Salt and pepper

Step by Step **1.** Fill a heat-resistant bowl with boiling water and drop **chicken pieces** into it. Let stand for 5 minutes; drain and pat dry.
2. In a saucepan, heat the **butter** or **peanut oil** and add **vinegar, tarragon,** and **mustard**.
3. Brush chicken with this mixture, sprinkle with **sugar**, and place skin side down on greased rack of broiling pan.
4. Place pan in lowest part of broiler. Broil about 20 minutes. Turn, baste with pan juices, and continue broiling until chicken is tender and skin is crisp and golden (about 20 more minutes).
5. Sprinkle with **salt and pepper** before serving.

Sugarless Catsup

In a large glass jar, combine **1 large can tomato paste,** ½ **cup cider vinegar,** ½ **cup water,** ½ **teaspoon salt,** **1 teaspoon oregano,** ⅛ **teaspoon cumin,** ⅛ **teaspoon nutmeg,** ¼ **teaspoon pepper,** ½ **teaspoon dry mustard,** and ½ **teaspoon minced garlic**. Cover tightly with a lid and store in the refrigerator until needed.

Coq au Vin

There are probably as many versions of this traditional favorite as there are French cooks. But the characteristic elements remain the same: onions and button mushrooms, a red wine sauce flavored with salt pork, and, contrary to what the name of the dish implies, "young" chickens.

Servings 8 to 10

Total Time ⏳ ⏳ ⏳

Major Utensils Large flameproof casserole
Large skillet

Ingredients
2 small chickens, skinned and cut in pieces (see page 4)
Salt and pepper
2 tablespoons butter
2 tablespoons oil
2 carrots, sliced
2 large onions, chopped
2 cups red wine
1 cup Brown Sauce (see page 11)
1 cup Chicken Stock (see page 10)
1 clove of garlic
1 shallot
Bouquet Garni (see page 110)
1 tablespoon tomato paste
¼ pound Blanched Salt Pork, diced (see page 21)
30 pearl onions, peeled
1 pound mushrooms, coarsely chopped

Step by Step

1. Season **chicken pieces** with **salt and pepper**. Sauté in casserole, over medium heat, in **butter** and **oil**. Remove from pan; set aside and keep hot.

2. In the remaining fat, gently sauté **carrots** and **chopped onion** (not pearl onions).

3. Return chicken to casserole, add **wine, Brown Sauce, Chicken Stock, garlic, shallot, Bouquet Garni, tomato paste**, salt, and pepper. Cover and bake at 350°F for about 1 hour 30 minutes.

4. Meanwhile, sauté **Blanched Salt Pork** in a skillet over medium heat until browned. Add **pearl onions** and **mushrooms,** and sauté lightly.

5. Remove chicken pieces from casserole. Strain sauce and return it to casserole along with the chicken, salt pork, pearl onions, and mushrooms. Cover and bake for a further 30 minutes. Serve very hot.

Crêpes à la King

Leftover chicken blended with veloutée sauce, enveloped in thin French pancakes, then covered with Mornay sauce form a dish fit for a king. The crêpes can be made in advance.

Servings	4 to 6
Total Time	⌛
Major Utensils	Crêpe pan Medium saucepan Casserole
Ingredients	1 cup cooked chicken, diced ½ cup Veloutée Sauce (see page 11) 1 cup Mornay Sauce (below)
Crêpes	1 cup flour Salt 1 cup milk 2 eggs 2 tablespoons butter, melted

Step by Step

1. To make the crêpe batter, mix the **flour** and **a pinch of salt** in a large bowl. Add the **milk** gradually, stirring with a wooden spoon or beating with a mixer. Add the **eggs** one by one. Stir in the **melted butter**. Set aside for at least 15 minutes.
2. Grease the crêpe pan lightly with vegetable oil and heat it. Pour a spoonful of batter onto it and swirl to coat the pan's surface. Cook over high heat until crêpe turns brown. Flip once. (Crêpes may be stored in the refrigerator until they are needed. Let them return to room temperature before handling them, or they will tear.)
3. Heat **Veloutée Sauce** in a saucepan. Add the **chicken** and heat through.
4. Put a large spoonful of this mixture on each crêpe. Roll up crêpes and place in a casserole. Cover with hot **Mornay Sauce** and brown under the broiler.

Mornay Sauce

Heat gently in a medium saucepan **1 cup of Veloutée Sauce** (see page 11). When it is hot, remove from the stove and blend in **½ cup of grated Parmesan or Gruyère cheese**. Stir until melted. Do not reheat.

Crunchy Almond Chicken

Almonds blended with garlic, ginger root, paprika, and cumin form the crunchy coating of this chicken dish. Bake potatoes with the chicken to save time.

Servings   4 to 6

Total Time   ⏳ ⏳

Major Utensils   Blender
                   Casserole

Ingredients
- 1 small chicken, cut in pieces (see page 4)
- 1 cup blanched slivered almonds
- 1 clove of garlic
- 1 thin slice of ginger root
- 1 teaspoon salt
- 1 teaspoon paprika
- ¼ teaspoon cumin, ground
- ¼ teaspoon pepper
- ½ cup butter, melted

Step by Step

1. Place **almonds, garlic,** and **ginger root** in blender; process until finely ground. Transfer to mixing bowl, and work in **salt, paprika, cumin,** and **pepper.**
2. Baste **chicken** with **melted butter**, and roll in almond mixture. Place skin side up in a casserole.
3. Bake at 375°F until tender, about 60 minutes.

🍲🍲🍲 Rich Pie Pastry

Measure **2 cups flour** without sifting. Add **½ tablespoon baking powder** and **a dash of salt;** stir to combine. Using two knives, cut **6 tablespoons shortening** into flour. Beat **½ cup cold water, 2 tablespoons vegetable oil,** and **1 small egg yolk** together. Make a well in flour mixture and add liquid. Mix well. Let pastry stand at room temperature for about 30 minutes before rolling out.

Curried Chicken

To "heat up" the ingredients of this recipe, simply add more curry powder. Boiled white rice is the traditional complement to zesty curry dishes.

Servings	4 to 6
Total Time	⏳ ⏳
Major Utensil	Flameproof casserole with cover
Ingredients	**1 large chicken, skinned and cut in pieces (see page 4)** **4 tablespoons butter or 2 tablespoons butter and 2 tablespoons oil** **2 onions, chopped** **1 tablespoon curry powder** **2 cups Chicken Stock (see page 10)** **1 cup White Sauce No. 2 (see page 11)** **Salt and pepper**
Step by Step	**1.** In a casserole, brown the **chicken pieces** in hot **butter** or **butter and oil**. **2.** Add the **chopped onions** and **curry powder;** stir thoroughly. Slowly add the **Chicken Stock**. **3.** Cover and bake at 350°F until chicken is tender (about 1 hour). Remove chicken; place on a platter and keep hot. **4.** Add **White Sauce** to the pan juices; mix thoroughly, cooking gently until sauce is hot. Strain and season with **salt** and **pepper**. **5.** Pour sauce over chicken. Serve with rice (below).

🍚🍚🍚 Boiled Rice

Put **1 cup of long-grain rice** in a saucepan and add **2 cups of water, ½ cup of butter,** and **salt**. Bring to boil over high heat, cover; reduce heat and cook gently until rice is tender (20–25 minutes). Rinse, drain, stir gently with a fork. Add more **butter,** to taste.

Teriyaki Chicken (see page 98). ▲
Chicken Chaud-froid (see page 26). ▶

Curried Chicken Salad

Curry powder is actually a blend of ground spices, such as cayenne pepper, turmeric, and fenugreek. Madras curries are far hotter than the Indonesian kind. Serve Curried Chicken Salad in lettuce cups.

Servings	4 to 6
Total Time	⏳
Major Utensils	2 mixing bowls
Ingredients	3 cups cooked chicken, cubed
	1 cup Mayonnaise (see page 42)
	2 teaspoons curry powder
	1 teaspoon salt
	1 cup celery, diced
	1 tart red-skinned apple, diced
	1 medium can mandarin oranges, drained; ¼ reserved for garnish
	½ cup cashew nuts, chopped
	Lettuce
Step by Step	**1.** Add **curry powder** and **salt** to **Mayonnaise** in a small bowl. More curry may be added for a stronger flavor.
	2. Combine **chicken, celery, apple, mandarin oranges,** and **cashews** in a bowl.
	3. Add mayonnaise curry to chicken and mix thoroughly. Serve on **lettuce cups** and garnish with **mandarin orange segments**.

🍳🍳🍳 Fried Onion Rings

Slice **onions** thickly. Dip into **milk**, then coat with **Seasoned Flour** (see page 28). Deep fry at 375°F until golden and crisp (about 3 minutes).

Deep-Fried Chicken

The backs and wings of a cut-up chicken do not always have adequate meat for deep frying. Halved breasts, legs, and thighs are best for coating with beer batter and immersing in hot oil.

Servings   4 to 6

Total Time   ⏳⏳⏳

Major Utensils   Deep fryer
Baking sheets

Ingredients   **1 small chicken, cut in pieces (see page 4) or 4 pounds chicken breasts, legs, and thighs**
Beer Batter (below)
Vegetable shortening for deep frying
Salt

Step by Step   **1.** Dip dry **chicken pieces** into **Beer Batter**.
2. Cook them, a few at a time, in a deep fryer filled with **vegetable shortening** heated to 375°F. Fry until chicken is cooked (about 15 minutes). Chicken is done if juices run clear when skin is pricked with a fork.
3. Transfer to baking sheets lined with paper towels, and keep warm until all pieces are cooked. Sprinkle with **salt** before serving.

🍲🍲🍲 Beer Batter

In a bowl, sift together **2 cups flour, 1 teaspoon salt,** and **1 teaspoon paprika**. In another bowl, beat together **2 eggs, 4 tablespoons corn or peanut oil,** and **2 cups flat beer**. Blend the two mixtures until smooth. Refrigerate for 2 hours, then stir again. Blend in **2 stiffly beaten egg whites** or **½ cup carbonated water**. Flavor with **curry powder, poultry seasoning, ground dill,** or **cumin**, if desired.

Deviled Chicken

In culinary terminology, a deviled dish is so highly seasoned that it tastes hot. For a more economical meal, use chicken legs. Boiled rice is the appropriate, bland complement to many deviled dishes.

Servings	6
Total Time	⏳
Major Utensil	Flameproof baking dish
Ingredients	**6 chicken breasts** **¼ cup butter** **½ cup honey** **¼ cup prepared mustard** **1 teaspoon salt** **1 teaspoon curry powder**
Step by Step	**1.** Melt **butter** in baking dish. Blend in **honey, mustard, salt,** and **curry powder** until smooth. **2.** Roll **chicken breasts** in butter mixture to coat completely. **3.** Arrange, meaty side up, in the pan and bake at 350°F until tender and richly glazed (about 45 minutes). Baste several times during baking.

Pie Pastry

Combine **2 cups sifted flour** and **½ teaspoon salt** in a large bowl. Cut in **4 tablespoons cold lard** and **4 tablespoons cold butter** until mixture resembles fine bread crumbs. Gradually add **2–3 tablespoons cold water**, mixing dough lightly with a fork until it forms a ball. Wrap in waxed paper, plastic wrap, or aluminum foil, and refrigerate or freeze until ready to use.

French Roasted Chicken

This is a reliable recipe for roasting a medium chicken. The cavity is stuffed with giblets, garlic, and thyme to impart delicious flavor.

Servings   4 to 6

Total Time   ⏳ ⏳ ⏳

Major Utensils Roasting pan
Trussing equipment

Ingredients
1 medium chicken with giblets
Salt and pepper
1 clove of garlic
¼ teaspoon thyme
2 tablespoons butter, softened
1 teaspoon dry mustard
1 cup cold liquid (water, stock, white wine, orange juice, or cream)

Step by Step
1. Remove extra fat from **chicken**; dice and pile in the middle of the roasting pan.
2. Salt and **pepper** chicken cavity. Place **giblets, garlic,** and **thyme** inside. Truss bird (see page 5). Rub a small amount of salt into the skin surface.
3. Blend **butter** and **mustard**; spread on chicken breast.
4. Set chicken on pile of fat. Roast in 350°F oven until chicken is tender (1½–2 hours).
5. Remove chicken from pan and place on a serving platter; keep warm.
6. To make gravy, place roasting pan over burner and heat until drippings bubble. Slowly add **cold liquid**; stir, and scrape bottom of pan. Bring to boil, strain, and serve with chicken.

To degrease pan juices, pour drippings into a steep-sided container. Place in freezer until fat rises; skim with a spoon or spatula. Alternatively, wrap ice cubes in cheesecloth and swirl quickly in the pan juices; the fat will congeal on the cloth.

Gardener's Chicken

There are hidden savings to this casserole. Because the vegetables are cooked with the chicken in the oven, there are few pots to clean at the end of the meal. A last-minute guest is easily accommodated by the addition of another potato or two, some 20 minutes before serving.

Servings   4 to 6

Total Time ⏳ ⏳

Major Utensils Large skillet
Casserole with cover

Ingredients
1 small chicken, cut in pieces (see page 4)
4-6 tablespoons unsalted butter
2 slices of bacon, chopped
2 large onions, thinly sliced
¼ pound mushrooms, sliced
2 stalks of celery, coarsely chopped
1 pound small new potatoes, peeled
½ pound turnips, peeled and sliced
1 large can tomatoes
Bouquet Garni (see page 110)
Salt and pepper

Garnish
Parsley, chopped
Rind of ½ orange, finely chopped

Step by Step

1. Melt the **butter** in a large skillet and sauté the **bacon, onions, mushrooms,** and **celery** for 5 minutes. Tip the pan to drain the butter to one side, remove the vegetables with a slotted spoon, and spread them over the bottom of a casserole.

2. Sauté the **chicken pieces** in the butter residue, adding a little more butter if necessary, until they are golden brown. Remove from the pan and place on bed of vegetables.

3. Add the **potatoes, turnips, tomatoes,** and **Bouquet Garni** to the casserole. Season with **salt and pepper** and cover the casserole with foil (so that no steam can escape) before putting the cover on. Cook on the middle shelf of a preheated oven at 300°F until meat is tender (about 1 hour 30 minutes).

4. Immediately before serving, sprinkle the **parsley** mixed with the **orange rind** over the casserole.

This recipe is illustrated on page 53.

Golden Baked Chicken

The chicken pieces are cooked in a hot oven while covered with foil. This method turns their skin crispy and brown, and is a good way to prepare chicken to serve cold at a picnic.

Servings 4

Total Time ⏳ ⏳

Major Utensil Shallow baking pan

Ingredients
1 small chicken, cut in pieces (see page 4)
1 egg
2 tablespoons water
2 teaspoons salt
½ teaspoon pepper
½ teaspoon basil
½ cup wheat germ or fine bread crumbs
2 tablespoons butter

Garnish **Parsley, chopped**

Step by Step
1. In a medium bowl, beat **egg** with **water**, **salt**, **pepper**, and **basil**.
2. Add **chicken pieces** and stir until coated.
3. Roll chicken in **wheat germ** or **bread crumbs**.
4. Grease baking pan with **butter**; place chicken on pan and dot with **remaining butter**. Cover with aluminum foil, and bake in 400°F oven until chicken is tender (about 1 hour).
5. Garnish with **parsley** before serving.

🍲🍲🍲 Chicken Coating Mix

In a small bowl combine **1½ cups dry bread crumbs, 1 cup flour, 4 tablespoons parsley flakes, 1 tablespoon paprika, 1 tablespoon onion powder, 2 teaspoons garlic powder, 1 teaspoon pepper, 1 tablespoon marjoram, 1 tablespoon thyme**, and **salt**, to taste. Blend in **¼ cup oil**. Store tightly covered until needed. To use, place moist chicken pieces in a bag containing mix. Shake bag to coat chicken. Bake on greased baking sheet at 400°F for 20 minutes. Turn, and cook for 10–20 more minutes, until chicken is tender.

Golden Glazed Broilers

The handsome golden glaze on these birds comes from condensed orange juice. For best results, cook on a covered barbecue.

Servings	4 to 6
Total Time	⏳ ⏳
Major Utensils	Barbecue with cover Trussing equipment
Ingredients	**2 very small chickens** **½ teaspoon rosemary or basil** **Vegetable oil** **1 small can frozen orange juice, thawed** **1 tablespoon soy sauce** **½ teaspoon ginger** **½ teaspoon salt** **2-3 oranges, thinly sliced**
Garnish	**Fresh mint**
Step by Step	**1.** Prepare barbecue for indirect cooking. **2.** Place **rosemary** or **basil** in **chicken** cavities. Truss birds firmly (see page 5). Rub outsides with **vegetable oil**. **3.** Prepare basting sauce by combining **orange juice, soy sauce, ginger**, and **salt** in a small bowl. Set aside. **4.** Place chicken on grill and cover barbecue. Cook for 50 minutes. **5.** Baste birds with orange mixture, and continue basting every 5 minutes until birds are tender (about 30 more minutes). **6.** Layer **orange slices** on a serving platter. Place chickens on oranges. Pour pan drippings over them. Garnish with a bouquet of **mint** in cavity openings before serving.

Mushrooms, peppers, and onions can be cooked on a greased grill above barbecue coals if covered with an inverted metal collander. Corn and potatoes can be wrapped in heavy aluminum foil and placed either on a grill or under the coals. Parboil potatoes and onions prior to barbecuing; otherwise they will burn before being cooked.

Hungarian Chicken

This recipe draws on an unusual combination of flavorings—from red currant jelly to orange juice.

Servings	4
Total Time	⏳ ⏳ ⏳
Major Utensils	Small saucepan Casserole with cover
Ingredients	**1 small chicken, cut in pieces (see page 4)** **¼ cup butter** **¼ cup Worcestershire sauce** **1 large clove of garlic, minced** **½ cup red currant jelly** **1 teaspoon ginger** **1 tablespoon Dijon mustard** **1 cup orange juice** **Tabasco sauce**
Step by Step	**1.** In a saucepan, heat **butter, Worcestershire sauce, garlic, red currant jelly, ginger, Dijon mustard, orange juice**, and 3 drops of **Tabasco sauce**. Stir while cooking until jelly is melted and sauce is smooth. **2.** Place **chicken** in casserole. Pour sauce over it and marinate 2–3 hours (all day, if convenient). **3.** Cover chicken and bake at 350°F for about 1 hour. **4.** Uncover and baste with pan juices. Continue cooking, uncovered, until golden brown, basting frequently.

Proceed sparingly with Tabasco sauce. Made from hot peppers, one extra drop can be too much. Worcestershire sauce, based on anchovy and chili, is strongly flavored, though less hot than Tabasco sauce.

Lemon-Chicken Catalan

This marriage of pot-roasted chicken with fresh lemon makes a delicious casserole. The Catalans serve it with broiled tomatoes, heavily sprinkled with minced chives, and hot French bread.

Servings   4 to 6

Total Time   ⌛ ⌛

Major Utensil   Deep skillet with cover

Ingredients
- 1 small chicken, cut in pieces (see page 4)
- 4 tablespoons butter
- Salt and pepper
- 2 or 3 cloves of garlic, crushed
- 3 lemons, thinly sliced
- ¼ teaspoon thyme
- 1 bay leaf
- 1 cup Chicken Stock (see page 10)
- 1 tablespoon cornstarch
- ¼ cup cold heavy cream

Step by Step

1. Heat **butter** in the skillet and brown **chicken pieces** in it. Sprinkle with **salt** and **pepper**. Add **garlic** and stir until brown.
2. Add **lemon** to chicken, along with **thyme** and **bay leaf**. Add **Chicken Stock** and bring to boil. Cover; cook over medium heat until chicken is tender, 40–60 minutes.
3. Place chicken on a deep, hot serving platter. Arrange lemon slices over chicken, but discard bay leaf and garlic. Keep warm.
4. Blend **cornstarch** with **cream**. Add to pan juices, and stir over medium heat until sauce is creamy and transparent. Strain the sauce over the chicken before serving.

Broiled Tomatoes

Slice firm **tomatoes** in half, crosswise. Sprinkle with **salt, pepper**, and **sugar**. Top with grated **Parmesan cheese** or **bread crumbs** and **minced chives**; dot with **butter**. Broil well below burner for 4–5 minutes.

Miniature Chicken Balls

Serve these appetizers on toothpicks as part of a buffet. Pineapple chunks, also on toothpicks, make tasty complements. Spicy sauces are delicious as dips.

Servings	2 to 4
Total Time	⏳
Major Utensil	Deep skillet or deep fryer
Ingredients	**1 cup cooked chicken, minced**
	1 cup White Sauce No. 4 (see page 11), cold
	1 egg, beaten
	Salt and pepper
	Soda cracker crumbs
	Vegetable oil or shortening for deep frying
Step by Step	**1.** Combine **White Sauce, chicken, farina, egg,** and **salt and pepper**, to taste.
	2. Shape into small balls and roll them in the **cracker crumbs**.
	3. Deep fry at 375°F until golden. Drain well and serve hot.

Deep frying fat will stay fresh longer if it is strained through cheesecloth after it has been used. An additional cup of fresh fat helps preserve shelf life. Never combine varieties of fat. Store tightly covered in a cool, dark place, if not in the refrigerator.

Mushroom-Chicken and Artichokes

A pound of mushrooms, lightly sautéed and blended with artichoke hearts and onion rings, is heaped onto a platter of golden chicken pieces before serving this dish.

Servings	4 to 6
Total Time	⌛ ⌛
Major Utensils	Ovenproof skillet with cover Large skillet
Ingredients	**2 small chickens, cut in pieces (see page 4)** ½ cup **butter** or ¼ cup **butter** and ¼ cup **oil** **Salt and pepper** 1 cup **Chicken Stock (see page 10)** 1 cup **Brown Sauce (see page 11)** 4 **artichoke hearts,** thinly sliced 1 pound **mushrooms,** thinly sliced 4 **onions,** sliced
Garnish	**Parsley,** chopped
Step by Step	**1.** Sauté **chicken pieces** in ¼ **cup butter** or **butter and oil** in the ovenproof skillet over medium heat until brown. Season with **salt and pepper**. Cover and bake at 325°F until chicken is tender (about 45 minutes). **2.** While chicken is cooking, sauté the **artichoke hearts** in **remaining butter** or **butter and oil** in the large skillet until tender. Remove from pan and keep warm. **3.** Adding fat as necessary, sauté the **mushrooms;** remove and set aside. Then sauté the **onions;** set aside. **4.** When chicken is ready, remove it from the skillet and keep hot. Add **Chicken Broth** to the pan and stir the chicken bits with a spoon to mix thoroughly. **5.** Add **Brown Sauce** and cook for a few minutes. **6.** Pour this sauce over the hot chicken, reserving any surplus in a side dish. Smother the chicken with artichokes, onions, and mushrooms. Sprinkle with **parsley**.

Orange-Glazed Chicken

Glazing a roasted chicken is a simple procedure that yields impressive results. Equally simple is adding almonds to the glaze and to the dressing—neither great skill nor expense is required.

Servings	6 to 8
Total Time	⏳ ⏳ ⏳
Major Utensils	Roasting pan Baking dish
Ingredients	**1 medium chicken, cut in pieces (see page 4)** **Salt and pepper** **Butter or oil** **Orange Glaze (below)** **Almond Dressing (see page 41)**
Step by Step	**1.** Season **chicken** pieces with **salt** and **pepper**, and brush with **butter** or **oil**. Place in roasting pan in center of oven, preheated to 350°F, and roast, basting frequently with the pan juices. **2.** While chicken is cooking, prepare **Almond Dressing**. Place in buttered baking dish and bake dressing after chicken has been cooking for 40 minutes. **3.** After chicken has cooked 1 hour 15 minutes, remove from oven and skim fat from pan juices. Return chicken to oven; roast for a further 15 minutes, basting frequently with **Orange Glaze,** until chicken is golden brown and tender. **4.** Remaining Orange Glaze may be poured over the chicken before serving, or passed separately. Serve glazed chicken with dressing.

Orange Glaze

Mix **2 tablespoons cornstarch, a pinch of ginger, 1½ cups orange juice**, and **1 cup corn syrup** in a small saucepan and cook over medium heat for 5–7 minutes, stirring constantly. Add **⅓ cup slivered almonds**.

Oriental Chicken

A wok is the preferred vessel for this recipe, although a large skillet will do nearly as well. Use wooden utensils (spoons or chopsticks) to stir-fry so that ingredients are not chopped during cooking. Serve with rice or noodles.

Servings	4 to 6
Total Time	⏳
Major Utensil	Wok
Ingredients	2-3 cups cooked chicken, cubed or shredded 2 tablespoons butter ½ pound mushrooms, sliced ½ pound snow peas ¾ cup Chicken Stock (see page 10) 1 small can water chestnuts, drained and thinly sliced ⅓ cup green onion, thinly sliced 2 tablespoons cornstarch 2 tablespoons soy sauce ¼ cup slivered almonds, toasted
Step by Step	**1.** Heat wok. Add **butter.** When melted, add **mushrooms.** Stir-fry until golden and limp. **2.** Add **snow peas** and ½ cup of Chicken Stock. Stir-fry for about 2 minutes. **3.** Add **water chestnuts, chicken,** and **green onion.** Stir-fry for about 1 minute. **4.** Combine **cornstarch, soy sauce,** and remaining Chicken Stock in a small bowl or a cup. Add to chicken mixture and stir, cooking until sauce boils and thickens. Garnish with toasted **almonds.**

To vary this recipe, use vegetable oil instead of butter, and stir-fry over high heat. Add minced garlic and diced celery; use peas or green beans instead of snow peas.

Oven-Poached Creamy Chicken

For a satisfying country-style meal, serve this dish with hot biscuits and cabbage and apple salad.

Servings   4 to 6

Total Time   ⏳ ⏳ ⏳

Major Utensil   Flameproof casserole with cover

Ingredients
- 1 small chicken
- 2 cloves
- 1 small onion
- 1 bay leaf
- 3 cups milk
- 1 stalk of celery with leaves, diced
- ¼ cup parsley, chopped
- ¼ teaspoon mace
- Salt and pepper
- 3 tablespoons butter, softened
- 3 tablespoons flour

Step by Step

1. Stick **cloves** in **onion**, and place in **chicken** cavity. Tie legs together loosely.
2. Place bird in casserole and put **bay leaf** on top. Add **milk, celery, parsley, mace, 2 teaspoons salt,** and **a dash of pepper.** Cover, and bake in 275°F oven until chicken is tender (2–3 hours).
3. Remove chicken and cut in pieces, discarding cloved onion and bay leaf. Place on a deep serving dish and keep warm.
4. Mix **butter** and **flour,** and add to casserole liquid. Cook over low heat, stirring constantly until sauce is thick and creamy. Season to taste with salt and pepper. Strain and pour over chicken before serving.

For perfect poaching, make sure the liquid cooks just under the boiling point. To shorten cooking time, bring the chicken and milk to simmer, uncovered on a burner, before placing in the oven; skim liquid, if necessary, beforehand.

Oyster-Chicken Casserole

Three steps—sautéing the vegetables, cooking the sauce, then blending chicken and oysters with the two—are all it takes to make a distinctive chicken dish to serve the most esteemed of guests.

Servings   6

Total Time   ⌛

Major Utensils   Medium skillet
Medium saucepan
Shallow casserole

Ingredients   **1 cup cooked chicken, diced**
1 cup oysters with liquor
⅓ cup dry, white vermouth, warmed
½ cup fine dry bread crumbs

Vegetable Mixture   **½ onion, finely chopped**
½ green pepper, finely chopped
¼ cup butter
½ pound mushrooms, halved or quartered
½ teaspoon salt
⅛ teaspoon black pepper

Sauce   **¼ cup butter**
¼ cup flour
¼ cup heavy cream
½ cup Chicken Stock (see page 10)
1 cup milk
⅛ teaspoon nutmeg
¾ teaspoon salt
⅛ teaspoon black pepper
2 tablespoons Parmesan cheese, grated

Step by Step

1. To prepare vegetable mixture, sauté **onion** and **green pepper** in **butter** in the skillet over low heat until onion is soft and golden. Add **mushrooms** and sauté for 5 minutes. Add **salt** and **pepper**. Set aside and keep warm.

2. To make the sauce, blend **flour** and **butter** together. Heat **cream, Chicken Stock, milk, nutmeg, salt,** and **pepper** in saucepan over medium heat. When warm, add the flour and butter, bit by bit, stirring over low heat with a whisk until smooth and thickened. Add **Parmesan cheese** and stir thoroughly.

3. Add **chicken, oysters with liquor,** vegetable mixture, and **vermouth** to the sauce. Pour into a well-greased casserole. Sprinkle with **bread crumbs** and bake at 400°F until bubbling and lightly browned (about 15 minutes).

Paella

Here's a hearty traditional Spanish dish that provides excellent fare for guests. In Spain paella is cooked in and served from a large two-handled iron pan (paella) from which the dish takes its name. For an authentic touch, use clean, unshucked clams and large, unshelled shrimp.

Servings 6 to 8

Total Time ⏳ ⏳

Major Utensils Large skillet
Heavy, shallow casserole with cover

Ingredients
1 medium chicken, cut in pieces (see page 4)
½ cup vegetable oil
3½ teaspoons salt
1½ cups rice
2 cloves of garlic, minced
1 bay leaf, crumbled
⅛ teaspoon saffron
¼ teaspoon pepper
1 cup canned tomatoes
3 cups water
1 green pepper, slivered
1 pimento, sliced
⅛ teaspoon cayenne
1 pound hot Italian sausage, cut in 1-inch pieces
1 dozen unshucked clams or 1 medium can clams
1 pound unshelled Prepared Shrimp, cooked (see page 34) or ½ pound cooked, shelled shrimp
1 cooked lobster tail, cut up
1 cup cooked green peas

Step by Step
1. In large skillet, brown **chicken pieces** in hot **oil**. Drain, sprinkle with **1 teaspoon of the salt,** then place in a casserole.
2. In the same skillet, add **rice** and **garlic** to the remaining oil and sauté until the rice is lightly browned. Add **remaining salt, the bay leaf, saffron, pepper, tomatoes, water, green pepper, pimento,** and **cayenne.** Bring to boil and pour over chicken. Cover tightly and bake at 400°F until rice is tender (25–30 minutes).
3. Meanwhile, sauté **sausage** in the skillet until browned; drain.
4. Add sausage, **clams, shrimp, lobster tail,** and **green peas** to chicken casserole, stirring lightly to mix. Reduce heat to 375°F and bake, covered, for 15 minutes.

Pineapple-Chicken Casserole

This casserole is made with 2 small chickens because they are likely to be more economical to buy than 1 large bird. Furthermore, the second one is a useful adjunct for serving cold on another day.

Servings   8

Total Time   ⏳ ⏳

Major Utensils   Shallow casserole
Medium saucepan

Ingredients
- 2 small chickens, quartered (see page 4)
- 2 teaspoons salt
- 1 tablespoon butter, melted
- 1 large can sliced pineapple in syrup
- 2 large cans yams in syrup
- 3 tablespoons cornstarch
- ¼ cup lemon juice
- ½ teaspoon ginger
- ½ teaspoon dry mustard
- 2 teaspoons onion, minced
- ½ cup red currant or apple jelly

Garnish   8 maraschino cherries with stems

Step by Step

1. Sprinkle **chicken** quarters with **1½ teaspoons salt** and place skin side up in the casserole. Brush with melted **butter**. Bake at 375°F for about 45 minutes.

2. Meanwhile, prepare sauce by draining syrup from **pineapple** and **yams** into the saucepan. Add **cornstarch, lemon juice, remaining salt, ginger, mustard,** and **onion,** and stir until well blended. Add **jelly** and stir constantly over medium–low heat until mixture thickens and comes to boil. Remove from heat.

3. When chicken has baked 45 minutes, drain juices from the pan.

4. Add pineapple slices and yams. Pour sauce over all. (May be prepared and refrigerated at this point.)

5. Return to oven and bake until tender (about 20 minutes). Serve garnished with **cherries**.

When roasting two chickens in a pan, be sure to leave room between the birds so they brown all over.

Quick Chicken Casserole

The short cooking time gives this casserole special appeal. It can be prepared in advance and then frozen until needed.

Servings	8
Total Time	⏳
Major Utensils	Large, deep skillet Casserole
Ingredients	2 cups cooked chicken, diced ¼ pound mushrooms, sliced or quartered 1 green pepper, diced ½ cup butter 4 tablespoons flour 2 cups milk 1¼ cups light cream 2 cups cooked noodles Salt and pepper 4 tablespoons dry sherry 2 tablespoons Parmesan cheese, grated
Step by Step	**1.** Sauté **mushrooms** and **green pepper** in **butter**. Add **flour** and simmer a few minutes, stirring constantly. Add **milk** and **cream,** stirring constantly until sauce comes to boil; reduce heat and continue cooking and stirring until thick and smooth. **2.** Add **chicken, noodles,** and **salt and pepper**, to taste; simmer 5 minutes. Remove from heat and add **sherry.** **3.** Place in greased casserole. Sprinkle with **Parmesan cheese** and bake at 350°F until golden and bubbling (about 20 minutes).

Roquefort Chicken

This recipe calls for Roquefort cheese, one of France's most famous fromages. When selecting Roquefort, make sure the cheese has a gray rind, and is evenly veined with blue. (If it is too white in appearance, or chalky in texture, it is not completely fermented.) Use blue cheese as an economical sustitute.

Servings 6

Total Time ⏳ ⏳

Major Utensils Medium saucepan
Baking dish with cover

Ingredients
6 chicken breasts, boned (see page 5)
2 cups water
½ cup wild rice
¼ teaspoon thyme
¼ teaspoon savory
¼ teaspoon rosemary
¼ teaspoon basil
Salt and pepper
¼ pound Roquefort cheese, cut in 12 sections
¼ cup butter, melted

Step by Step

1. In a medium saucepan, boil **water** to which ½ **teaspoon salt** has been added. Add **wild rice**. Cook until just tender (about 20 minutes). Drain.
2. Add **thyme, savory, rosemary**, and **basil**. Stir well and set aside.
3. Season **chicken breasts** with **salt and pepper**. Place 1 section of **Roquefort cheese** on each piece of chicken. Top with 1 tablespoon rice per breast. Fold chicken in half and fasten with toothpicks.
4. Place chicken in greased baking dish. Brush with **melted butter**. Cover and bake 40–45 minutes at 380°F.
5. Remove cover and top chicken with **remaining 6 sections of cheese**. Broil until cheese melts and chicken turns golden, about 5 minutes.

There will be about ¾ cup of wild rice left over in this recipe. Combine it with boiled white or brown rice to serve as a side dish, or save for adding to soup.

Spiced Chicken and Rice

Despite its elaborate appearance, this Indonesian dish takes about 35 minutes of preparation time. Side dishes of vegetables, fruits, and nuts should be chosen for contrast in flavor and color.

Servings	6 to 8
Total Time	⏳ ⏳ ⏳
Major Utensils	Large, deep skillet with cover Large saucepan with cover
Ingredients	1 small chicken 1 pound onions: 1 whole; remainder thinly sliced 1 bay leaf 1 sprig of parsley Salt and pepper 2 cups long-grain rice 3 tablespoons olive or vegetable oil 2 tablespoons peanut butter 1 teaspoon chili powder ¼ pound Prepared Shrimp, shelled (see page 34) ¼ pound ham, diced 1 teaspoon cumin, crushed 1½ teaspoons coriander seed, crushed 1 clove of garlic, crushed Mace
Garnish	½ cucumber, unpeeled, sliced 2 hard-cooked eggs, cut into wedges 8–12 cooked Prepared Shrimp, unshelled (see page 34)
Side Dishes	Apricot-and-mango chutney Sliced tomatoes, dressed with sugar and lemon juice Oranges, peeled and sliced Green peppers, sliced, with raw onion rings Red peppers, sliced, with raw onion rings Pineapple, cut in chunks Bananas, sliced and fried Coconut, shredded and toasted Almonds or cashews, sautéed in butter
Step by Step	**1.** Place **chicken** in skillet, with **1 whole, peeled onion**, the **bay leaf**, and the **parsley sprig**. Add a seasoning of **salt and pepper**, and enough cold water to cover the chicken. Bring to boil over medium heat, remove any scum, then reduce the heat. Cover and simmer until the chicken is tender (about 1 hour).

Step by Step continued

2. While chicken cooks, prepare a selection of side dishes. Set aside.
3. Lift out the chicken and allow to cool slightly.
4. Strain the broth through a fine sieve. Bring 4 cups of it to boil in the saucepan then add the **rice**; cover and cook gently until the rice is just tender (about 25 minutes). Drain the rice thoroughly in a colander and cover with a dry cloth.
5. Remove the skin from the chicken and cut the meat into small pieces.
6. Heat the **oil** in the skillet and sauté the **remaining onions** over low heat until they begin to color. Stir in the **peanut butter** and **chili powder**. Add the **shrimp, ham**, chicken, and finally the rice, which should now be dry and fluffy.
7. Continue to sauté over low heat, stirring frequently, until the rice is slightly brown. Add the **cumin, coriander seed**, and the **garlic**, and stir them with **a pinch of mace** into the rice. Season the mixture to taste with salt.
8. Pile the rice and chicken mixture on a hot serving dish and garnish with **cucumber slices, egg wedges**, and large **shrimp**.
9. Serve Spiced Chicken and Rice with a number of small side dishes around the chicken.

Onions can be peeled and sliced without inducing tears if they are parboiled for about 8 seconds. Any onion odor left on hands or cutting board can be removed by rubbing with lemon juice or dry mustard, before washing.

Sugar-Broiled Chicken

Scandinavians are masters in the art of using sugar with their food. This chicken is an excellent example. Serve with broiled tomatoes and parslied rice.

Servings 4

Total Time ⏳ ⏳

Major Utensil Broiling pan

Ingredients
1 small chicken, cut in pieces (see page 4)
1 lemon: rind grated off, then cut in half
3 teaspoons salt
½ teaspoon pepper
1 teaspoon paprika
½ cup butter, melted, or ¼ cup butter
 and ¼ cup chicken fat, melted together
2 tablespoons sugar

Step by Step

1. Place the **chicken pieces** in bottom of broiling pan. Rub and squeeze the **lemon halves** over the chicken. Combine the **salt, pepper**, and **paprika** and sprinkle on top of chicken.

2. Brush both sides of chicken with **¼ cup butter**, or **butter and chicken fat**. Arrange the pieces skin side down and sprinkle with **1 tablespoon sugar**.

3. Place broiler pan in the lowest part of the preheated broiler. Broil on one side for 30 minutes.

4. Turn chicken and baste with **remaining butter**, and sprinkle with the **rest of the sugar**. Broil for another 15 minutes. Decrease the heat if the skin is browning too rapidly. Continue broiling for 15 more minutes, or until skin is crisp and golden.

Substitute 2 very small chickens cut in half for the chicken pieces in this recipe. Or, use drumsticks and thighs from a medium chicken.

Tarragon Chicken

An aromatic herb that flourishes in Europe, Asia, and the Americas, tarragon does subtle wonders for chicken. Fresh tarragon can be used in place of dried tarragon, but because the flavor is less concentrated, use three times the amount.

Servings 4

Total Time ⏳ ⏳

Major Utensil Casserole with cover

Ingredients
- **1 small chicken, cut in pieces (see page 4)**
- **Salt and pepper**
- **1 teaspoon tarragon**
- **Paprika**
- **1 onion, sliced**
- **3 potatoes, cubed**
- **4 carrots, sliced**
- **2 stalks of celery, sliced**

Step by Step

1. Season **chicken** with **salt, pepper,** and **tarragon.** Place in casserole and dust with **paprika.** Roast at 400°F, uncovered, for 15 minutes.

2. Add the **onion, potatoes, carrots,** and **celery.** Cover and return to the oven until meat and vegetables are tender (about 45 minutes).

Make tarragon-flavored chicken soup by preparing Chicken Stock (see page 10) with the carcass remaining from this dish. Do not hesitate to include bones and meat left on plates; they will become sterilized while simmering. Add rice and vegetables after stock has been degreased; season with tarragon, if necessary.

Teriyaki Chicken

Although Oriental in origin, this recipe can be made from ingredients found in most grocery stores. Broiling enhances the nut-like flavor of the sesame-seed coating.

Servings 4

Total Time ⏳ ⏳ ⏳

Major Utensil Broiling pan

Ingredients
1 small chicken, split or disjointed (see page 4)
1–1½ tablespoons sesame seeds

Marinade
¼ cup sake or sherry
¼ cup oil
¼ cup soy sauce
1 clove of garlic, crushed
1 teaspoon ginger

Step by Step **1.** Prepare the marinade by combining the **sake** or **sherry, oil, soy sauce, garlic,** and **ginger.** Pour over the **chicken** and marinate for 2 hours. Turn the chicken occasionally to keep the pieces well coated.
2. Broil 5–6 inches from the burner, basting frequently with the marinade and turning the chicken every 5–10 minutes.
3. When almost done, dip each piece of chicken in the marinade, roll thoroughly in **sesame seeds,** and return to the broiler to brown. Watch the chicken carefully to make sure that the sesame seeds do not burn.

This recipe is illustrated on page 71.

Zucchini-Chicken with Orange

Zucchini cooked with citrus fruit is an unusual combination. Serve this chicken dish with plain vegetables, such as boiled rice and green beans, that complement the tangy chicken.

Servings	4 to 6
Total Time	⏳ ⏳
Major Utensils	Flameproof casserole with cover Large skillet
Ingredients	**2 medium chickens, cut in pieces (see page 4)** **½ cup butter or ¼ cup butter and ¼ cup oil** **1 pound zucchini, sliced** **4 oranges: 1 juiced, 3 sliced** **1 lemon: ½ juiced, ½ sliced** **1 cup white wine** **1 cup Brown Sauce (see page 11)** **Salt and pepper** **Paprika**
Step by Step	1. In a flameproof casserole, sauté **chicken pieces** in ¼ **cup butter,** or **butter and oil,** over medium heat until brown. Cover and bake at 325°F until chicken is tender (about 45 minutes). 2. About 10 minutes before the chicken is ready, sauté the **zucchini slices** in **remaining butter** in a skillet, remove from pan and keep warm. Sauté the **slices of lemon** and **orange;** keep warm. 3. When chicken is ready, remove from the casserole and set aside; keep warm. 4. Add **white wine** to the pan and mix with pan juices. Boil liquid to reduce by half. 5. Add **Brown Sauce, orange juice,** and **lemon juice.** Season with **salt, pepper,** and **paprika,** to taste. 6. To serve, place chicken on a platter and surround it with the zucchini, oranges, and lemon. Serve gravy as a side dish.

Young zucchini, up to 6 inches long, are considered the best for cooking. Larger zucchini tend to be watery.

Chicken Liver Pâté

A pâté recipe this simple to prepare is reason enough to try it. That it is highly nutritious—a good source of iron and Vitamin A, for starters—is further inducement to serve this appetizer.

Servings 6

Total Time ⏳

Major Utensils Large skillet
Food mill
6 small bowls

Ingredients **1 pound chicken livers, cut in large pieces**
1 onion, chopped
2/3 cup butter: 1/3 cup softened, 1/3 cup melted
1/4 cup cognac
Salt and pepper

Step by Step **1.** In a large skillet, sauté the **chopped onion** over medium heat until soft. Add the **chicken livers** and sauté lightly. Their interiors should be pink.
2. Put the liver through a food mill (do not use a blender) or mash with a fork until coarse. Add **softened butter, cognac, salt,** and **pepper;** mix well. Fill small bowls and let cool.
3. Coat each bowl of liver with a thin layer of **melted butter.** This pâté will keep for several days in the refrigerator.

Chicken livers will have a bitter aftertaste unless all white, stringy pieces have been removed prior to cooking. Any discolored sections should also be cut away.

Chicken Livers with Grapes

Never underestimate the chicken liver—especially when prepared with a wine sauce flavored with green grapes. Whether fresh or frozen, chicken livers are inexpensive and nutritious, easy to prepare and fast to cook.

Servings   6

Total Time   ⌛

Major Utensil   Large skillet

Ingredients
- 1½ pounds chicken livers
- Salt and pepper
- ¾ pound seedless green grapes
- 6 slices of white bread, crusts removed
- ¾ cup butter
- 2 tablespoons vegetable oil
- ⅓–½ cup Madeira, port, or sherry

Step by Step

1. Season the **chicken livers** with **salt and pepper**; set aside.
2. Melt **¼ cup of the butter** in a skillet, together with the **oil**. When hot, sauté the **bread** golden brown on both sides. Remove from pan and keep warm in the oven.
3. Melt the **remaining butter** in the skillet and sauté the livers for 3–5 minutes on each side; they should be slightly pink in the center. Remove the livers from the pan and keep warm.
4. Stir the **wine** into the pan juices and reduce by rapid boiling until the sauce has thickened to a syrupy consistency. Add the **grapes** to the sauce and heat them through.
5. To serve, arrange the sautéed bread on a serving dish, top with chicken livers, and spoon the grapes and sauce over them. Serve the livers immediately, before the sauce soaks into the bread.

This recipe is illustrated on page 143.

Sweet and Sour Chicken Livers

Chicken livers are more popular than other livers because they are tender and mildly flavored. Served with sweet and sour sauce, they are likely to please even antiliver diehards. Rice goes well with this dish.

Servings	4
Total Time	⌛
Major Utensil	Wok
Ingredients	1 pound chicken livers 4 cups water 1 teaspoon salt 2 slices of ginger root 1 tablespoon brandy Oil for deep frying Sweet and Sour Sauce (below)
Step by Step	**1.** In the wok, bring **water** to a boil. Add ½ **teaspoon salt, ginger root,** and **livers.** Parboil 1½–2 minutes. Drain livers well. **2.** In a bowl, mix livers with ½ **teaspoon salt** and **brandy.** Let stand 30 minutes, stirring occasionally. **3.** Meanwhile, prepare **Sweet and Sour Sauce.** Set aside and keep warm. **4.** Fill wok with oil and heat to 375°F. Deep fry livers until golden brown. Remove with slotted spoon and drain well. **5.** Pour Sweet and Sour Sauce over livers; if rice is served as a side dish, pour sauce over all.

🍲🍲🍲 Sweet and Sour Sauce

In a saucepan, combine ¼ **cup water,** 2 **tablespoons catsup,** 2 **tablespoons brandy,** 1 **tablespoon soy sauce,** 1 **teaspoon brown sugar,** and ½ **teaspoon cornstarch.** Bring to boil, stirring until sauce thickens.

Cornish Hen with Sausage

Cornish hens are wrapped in bacon and baked with knockwurst in this hearty dish. Pork (breakfast) sausages are first browned, then added in the final cooking step.

Servings	4
Total Time	⏳ ⏳ ⏳
Major Utensils	Large skillet Casserole with cover
Ingredients	**4 Cornish hens** **Salt and pepper** **4 slices of bacon** **3 sprigs of parsley** **1 teaspoon thyme** **2 bay leaves** **1 clove of garlic** **1 small onion, sliced** **2 carrots, sliced** **1 cup water** **1 pound knockwurst** **2 tablespoons wine vinegar** **2 tablespoons sugar** **4 pork sausages**
Step by Step	**1.** Season **Cornish hens** with **salt** and **pepper**. Wrap 1 slice of **bacon** around each hen and fasten with a toothpick. In a skillet over medium heat, brown hens on all sides. **2.** Tie the herbs, **parsley, thyme, bay leaves**, and **garlic,** in cheesecloth, and place in casserole along with Cornish hens. Add **onion, carrots, water, knockwurst, wine vinegar,** and **sugar**; stir. Cover, and bake at 375°F for about 1 hour 30 minutes. **3.** Meanwhile, brown **pork sausages**. **4.** Remove casserole from oven. Take out bag of herbs; add sausages. Return casserole to oven, and bake uncovered for about 30 minutes.

Duck Breasts in Pastry

This impressive dish can be started the day before serving by roasting the bird and preparing the stuffing. Use leftover meat to make duck pâté.

Servings 12

Total Time ⏳⏳⏳

Major Utensils Roasting pan
Large skillet
Baking sheet

Ingredients
3 ducks
4 tablespoons lean bacon, chopped
2 duck livers, chopped
4 tablespoons onion, finely chopped
Rind of 1 orange, grated
2 tablespoons butter
3 tablespoons green olives, chopped
1 tablespoon brandy
1½ pounds prepared puff pastry
1 large egg, beaten

Step by Step
1. Place **ducks** in roasting pan and bake at 400°F for 45–60 minutes. Set aside to cool.
2. In a large skillet, sauté the **bacon, duck livers, onions,** and **orange rind** in the **butter**. Add the **olives**, moistened with **brandy**, and cook over moderate heat for about 5 minutes.
3. Skin the ducks and carve off the breasts, leaving each whole. Cut each breast into 2 portions.
4. Roll out the **puff pastry** ¼ inch thick and divide into 12 pieces.
5. Lay a portion of duck on each pastry square, spread a little of the bacon mixture on top, and wrap the pastry around meat.
6. Seal the seams with **egg** and place the envelopes, seams up, on a moistened, floured baking sheet. Brush with egg and bake at 400°F until pastry is golden, about 25 minutes.

🍲🍲🍲 Duck Pâté

Coarsely grind **duck meat** remaining on carcasses along with remaining **duck liver**. Blend in **2 cups ground veal, 1 cup white bread crumbs, 2 tablespoons finely chopped onion, ½ teaspoon dried chervil,** and **3 tablespoons chopped parsley.** Season to taste with **salt and pepper.** Stir in the **grated rind of 1 orange** and **2 tablespoons brandy** or **dry sherry.** Add **2 lightly beaten eggs.** Spoon the pâté into a buttered terrine and cover with **bacon slices.** Place in a roasting pan half-filled with boiling water. Bake at 325°F for 1 hour 15 minutes.

This recipe is illustrated on page 89.

Duck in Orange Sauce

Two ducks are called for in this version of roast duck with orange. The sauce is made with giblet stock and curaçao, a sweet liqueur made from bitter oranges.

Servings 6 to 8

Total Time ⏳ ⏳

Major Utensils Roasting pan
Medium saucepan

Ingredients
2 ducks (4–5 pounds each), trussed (see page 5)
4 oranges: peeled and sectioned; juice reserved; rind cut into strips
1 tablespoon sugar
½ cup red wine vinegar
1¼ cups Giblet Stock (below)
Juice of ½ lemon (1½ tablespoons)
1 tablespoon arrowroot
1 tablespoon water
3 tablespoons curaçao

Step by Step

1. Place the **trussed ducks** on their sides in greased roasting pan. Cook in an oven at 400°F for 40 minutes, then turn the ducks over and cook for another 30 minutes. Finally, place the ducks on their backs and cook for a final 30 minutes. Baste frequently.

2. Meanwhile, in a small saucepan, boil the **orange rind strips** for 10 minutes in a little water. Drain them and set aside, with the **orange segments,** for garnishing.

3. About 15 minutes before duck is cooked, boil the **sugar** and **vinegar** in a medium saucepan until reduced to a light caramel. Add the **Giblet Stock, lemon juice,** and **reserved orange juice** and boil for 5 minutes.

4. Blend **arrowroot** with **water** into a paste and add to sauce. Stir until thick and shiny.

5. Strain the sauce, stir in the **curaçao,** and pour over the cooked duck. Garnish with orange rind and segments.

Giblet Stock

Place **poultry neck** and **giblets** (heart and gizzard) in a large saucepan. Add **1 chopped onion** and **1 chopped stalk of celery**. Cover with cold water; simmer for one hour.

This recipe is illustrated on page 107.

Duck in Wine Sauce

For robust flavor, use full-bodied dry red wine. Since cream is an ingredient, the pan juices must be carefully degreased, lest the sauce be too rich.

Servings	4 to 6
Total Time	⌛ ⌛ ⌛
Major Utensil	Ovenproof skillet with cover
Ingredients	**1 duck (about 5 pounds), cut in pieces (see page 4)** **Salt and pepper** **½ pound pearl onions** **¾ pound mushrooms, quartered if large** **2 green onions, chopped** **2 cups red wine** **1 cup light cream**
Garnish	**Parsley, chopped**
Step by Step	**1.** Season **duck pieces** with **salt** and **pepper**. In skillet, brown over high heat (no fat is needed). **2.** Add **pearl onions** and **mushrooms**. Cover, and bake at 350°F until duck is tender (approximately 2 hours). **3.** Arrange duck and vegetables on serving platter, and keep hot. **4.** Pour off pan juices, degrease, and return to pan. Add **green onions** and **red wine**. Stir to blend thoroughly. Boil sauce until reduced by half. **5.** Add **cream** to the sauce to thicken. Sprinkle with **parsley**.

Duck in Orange Sauce (see page 105). ▶

Duck in the Apple Orchard

Apples, apple juice, and applejack are the "orchard" for which this dish is named. Green peas or beans are good vegetables for complementing the flavor of apples and duck.

Servings	8
Total Time	⏳ ⏳ ⏳
Major Utensil	Large, ovenproof skillet with cover
Ingredients	**2 ducks (5 pounds each), quartered (see page 5)**
	2 onions, chopped
	2 carrots, chopped
	3 cloves
	6 tablespoons applejack
	2 cups apple juice
	16 apple slices, cored
	½ cup butter
Step by Step	1. In a skillet, brown **duck pieces** (no fat is necessary). Pour off fat.

2. Add **onions, carrots**, and **cloves** to the duck.
3. Pour **applejack** over bird. Heat, and ignite.
4. When flames die down, add **1 cup of apple juice**.
5. Cover, and bake in 325°F oven until duck is tender (about 1 hour). Check occasionally, and add more apple juice if ingredients are drying, or browning too quickly.
6. Remove duck from pan. Strain pan juices into a heat-resistant container. Cool duck and juices; refrigerate at least one hour.
7. Skim fat from juices. Strain liquid into a large measuring cup. If less than two cups, add **more apple juice** to make up the difference.
8. Return duck and pan juices to the skillet. Place in oven and heat at 325°F until liquid simmers and duck is very hot.
9. Meanwhile, sauté **apple slices** lightly in **butter**.
10. Spoon pan juices over duck and garnish with apple slices before serving.

Duck with Green Peas

A garnish of peas adds a final touch to braised duck, in itself a relatively uncomplicated dish that nonetheless is guest fare.

Servings	4 to 6
Total Time	⏳ ⏳
Major Utensils	Large, ovenproof skillet with cover Medium skillet
Ingredients	1 duck (5 pounds), trussed (see page 5) Salt and pepper 30 pearl onions, or 6 medium onions, chopped ½ pound Blanched Salt Pork, diced (see page 21) 1 cup Chicken Stock (see page 10) 2 cups Brown Sauce (see page 11) Bouquet Garni (below)
Garnish	2 cups large green peas
Step by Step	**1.** Season **duck** with **salt and pepper.** Put in the large skillet and brown over high heat (no fat is necessary). Remove duck from the pan and keep warm. **2.** Brown **Blanched Salt Pork** and **onions** in the medium skillet. Drain onions and set aside. **3.** Degrease duck juices, then add **Chicken Stock.** Stir thoroughly. Blend in **Brown Sauce.** Return duck to pan along with **Bouquet Garni** and onions. Cover, and bake at 350°F until duck is tender (approximately 1 hour). **4.** Meanwhile, steam-cook **green peas** until just tender (approximately 25 minutes if fresh, 15 minutes if frozen, and 10 minutes if canned). Peas should be cooked when duck is. **5.** Arrange duck and onions on a serving platter. Pour sauce over all. Garnish with peas.

Bouquet Garni

Used for flavoring soups, stews, sauces, and braised foods, a Bouquet Garni is composed of **2 sprigs of parsley,** ½ **bay leaf,** and **1 sprig** or ⅛ **teaspoon of thyme.** The herbs are immersed in the liquid, tied together or contained in a small cloth sack.

Duck with Peaches

Broiled peaches and peach brandy flavored sauce smother roast duck with tangy sweetness in this relatively uncomplicated recipe.

Servings	4 to 5
Total Time	⏳ ⏳
Major Utensils	Roasting pan Medium saucepan Broiling pan
Ingredients	**1 duck (4-5 pounds), trussed (see page 5)** **Salt and pepper** **1 tablespoon butter** **3 green onions, chopped** **1 can large peach halves, liquid reserved** **¼ cup peach brandy** **1 cup Brown Sauce (see page 11)** **¼ cup currant jelly** **Icing sugar**
Step by Step	**1.** Season **duck** with **salt** and **pepper,** and place in a roasting pan. Roast at 375°F until tender (approximately 1 hour 30 minutes). **2.** Meanwhile, in a saucepan, lightly brown **green onions** in **butter.** Add **peach liquid** and **peach brandy.** Boil to reduce sauce by half. **3.** Add **Brown Sauce** and **currant jelly** to the sauce, and bring to boil. Remove from burner, but keep hot. **4.** Place **peaches** on a broiling pan and dust with **icing sugar.** Broil until golden brown. **5.** Cut duck in pieces, and arrange on a hot serving platter. Garnish with peaches. Pour some of the sauce over duck; serve the remainder separately.

Most of what is called peach brandy in North America is actually peach-flavored cordial. Genuine peach brandy is distilled from the fruit; it is commonly produced in France.

111

Duck with Turnip

Few vegetables go better with duck than turnip and onions. In this recipe, they are lightly sautéed, then added to the bird at the last cooking step to be braised in wine sauce.

Servings 4 to 6

Total Time ⏳ ⏳ ⏳

Major Utensils Roasting pan
Medium skillet

Ingredients
1 duck (about 5 pounds), trussed (see page 5)
Salt and pepper
1 pound turnip, diced (2 cups)
1 teaspoon sugar
20 pearl onions
1 cup butter
1 cup white wine
2 cups Brown Sauce (see page 11)
Bouquet Garni (see page 110)

Step by Step
1. Season **duck** with **salt** and **pepper,** and place in a roasting pan. Roast at 350°F for 1 hour 30 minutes.
2. Meanwhile, in a skillet over medium heat, sauté diced **turnip** lightly in ½ **cup butter.** Sprinkle with **sugar.** Remove from pan and set aside.
3. Sauté **pearl onions** lightly in **remaining butter.** Set aside.
4. Remove cooked duck from pan and set aside. Degrease pan juices. Add **white wine** and blend thoroughly. Boil until sauce is reduced by half.
5. Add **Brown Sauce** and **Bouquet Garni** and return duck to sauce. Cover, and bake for 20 minutes.
6. Add turnip and onions, and continue baking until duck is tender (about 45 minutes).
7. Place duck on serving platter, and arrange turnip and onions around it. Moisten with sauce, and serve remaining sauce separately.

🍲🍲🍲 Duck with Olives

Substitute ½ **pound pitted black or stuffed green olives** for the turnip in the recipe above. Add to the duck with the onions (Step 6).

Duck with Vegetables

Although this is a complicated recipe, most of the work can be done while the duck is roasting. No side dishes are necessary.

Servings	4 to 6
Total Time	⌛ ⌛ ⌛
Major Utensils	Roasting pan with rack Trussing equipment (see page 5) Stockpot
Ingredients	**1 duck (5 pounds)** **3 celery stalks with leaves, halved** **2 onions, halved** **1 apple, quartered** **1 cup Giblet Stock (see page 105)** **1 cup dry red wine** **4 carrots, cut into thin strips** **2 celery knobs, thinly sliced** **2 long potatoes, cut into thin strips** **1 pound whole green beans** **4 leeks, cut in half lengthwise** **4 tablespoons honey or strained orange marmalade**
Garnish	**½ cup parsley, chopped**
Step by Step	**1.** Put **celery stalks, onions,** and **apple** in duck cavity. Truss (see page 5). **2.** Place breast down on a rack in the roasting pan. Prick skin all over to release fat. Roast at 325°F for 20 minutes, then turn bird onto its side. Prick skin and roast for 20 minutes longer. Turn onto the other side, prick skin and roast for 20 more minutes. Finally, turn bird breast up, prick, and roast an additional 20 minutes. **3.** Drain fat, and roast 40 minutes longer, basting frequently with **Giblet Stock** blended with **wine.** **4.** About 25 minutes before duck is cooked, fill a stockpot with water and bring to boil. At the same time, wrap **carrots, celery knobs, potatoes, beans,** and **leeks** separately in cheesecloth. **5.** Immerse carrots, then celery knobs in boiling water; cook for 5 minutes. Add potatoes, beans, and leeks. Continue boiling until all vegetables are tender (about 10 minutes). **6.** Meanwhile raise oven temperature to 400°F and baste duck with **honey** or **orange marmalade** to bronze the skin. Bake for about 10 minutes, or until duck is tender. **7.** Remove trussing string, pour juices from cavity into the pan, discarding the other ingredients. **8.** Arrange duck on a large platter and surround with vegetables. Boil down pan juices a few minutes, degrease, and spoon juice over bird and vegetables. Garnish with **parsley** before serving.

Peking Duck

The essence of Peking Duck is its crisp skin, which is stripped off the cooked duck before being served. Preparations for this famous dish are elaborate, as is the ceremony for eating it.

Servings	4 to 6
Total Time	⏳ ⏳ ⏳
Major Utensils	Rod or broom handle Electric fan Griddle Roasting pan Small saucepan
Ingredients	**1 large duck (5-6 pounds)** **2 tablespoons brandy, vodka, or gin (optional)** **18 green onions, trimmed 3-4 inches long**
Pancakes	**4 cups all-purpose flour** **2½ cups water** **2 tablespoons sesame seed oil**
Table Sauce	**5 tablespoons plum sauce** **2 teaspoons sugar** **2 teaspoons sesame seed oil** **1 tablespoon cold water**
Basting Sauce	**4 tablespoons soy sauce** **1½ tablespoons superfine sugar** **½ cup cold water**
Step by Step	**1.** The skin of the uncooked **duck** should be thoroughly dried. Wipe and dry the duck and pass a length of string under the wings so that it can be suspended from a rod or broom handle placed across the seats of two chairs. Set a plate under the duck to catch any drips. Rubbing the skin with the **brandy, vodka,** or **gin** aids the drying process. **2.** Direct a blast of air at the duck from an electric fan and let it dry for at least 3-4 hours. Alternatively, hang the duck for 8 hours or overnight in a drafty place. **3.** Use a sharp knife to make two cuts ½-¾ inch long at the bulb end of each **green onion,** then make two similar cuts at right angles to the first cuts. Put the green onions in a large bowl of ice water and leave in the refrigerator until required. The cut ends of each green onion will fan out to resemble a brush. **4.** To make the Pancakes, bring 2½ cups of **water** to boil. Meanwhile, sift the **flour** into a bowl. Then, mixing all the time, gradually add only enough of the boiling water to make a soft dough that leaves the sides of the bowl clean. Knead the dough for 10 minutes on a lightly floured surface until it becomes rubbery. Cover with a cloth and let stand for at least 20 minutes.

Step by Step Continued

5. Roll the dough out, ¼ inch thick, and cut it into rounds (about 28) with a plain 2-inch cookie cutter. Brush the top of half the rounds with **sesame seed oil** and place an unbrushed round on top. Roll out each pair of pancakes (about 14), as thinly as possible, to a diameter of about 6 inches.

6. Heat an ungreased griddle or heavy skillet for 30 seconds, then lower the heat. Put in the first pair of pancakes, turning when bubbles appear on the surface and the underside is flecked with brown and looks floury. Cook all the pancakes in this way (they may puff up into balloons), and allow them to cool. Wrap the cooked pancakes in several foil packages and store them in the refrigerator until needed.

7. Mix **soy sauce** and **superfine sugar** with ½ cup of **cold water** to make the Basting Sauce. Brush the sauce all over the duck. Place the duck, breast upward, on a wire rack in a roasting pan. Pour in enough boiling water to reach ¼ inch up the sides of the pan. Roast the duck in the lower part of a preheated oven at 400°F for 45 minutes, brushing with the basting sauce every 15 or 20 minutes. Turn up the heat to 450°F and roast for a further 45 minutes.

8. To make the Table Sauce, mix the **plum sauce, sugar,** and **sesame seed oil** together in the small pan, add 1 tablespoon of **cold water** and bring the sauce to boil; stir over low heat for 2–3 minutes. Pour the sauce into a serving bowl.

9. Put the packages of prepared pancakes into the oven to reheat.

10. To assemble the final dish, cut off the duck skin with scissors or a sharp knife, in 1- or 2-inch squares; place on a serving dish and keep warm.

11. Carve the meat into long, thin slivers and arrange on another dish to keep warm.

12. Pile the pancakes on a hot dish and cover with a napkin or folded cloth to keep them warm.

13. Put the green onion brushes in a bowl and arrange all these dishes, with the Table Sauce, on the table.

14. To eat, carefully pull the two halves of a pancake apart, starting where the seam can be seen quite clearly. Dip a green onion brush in the sauce and brush it liberally onto the soft moist side of the open pancake. Top with pieces of the duck skin and slivers of meat; carefully fold and roll up the pancake.

This recipe is illustrated on page 125.

Goose in Orange Sauce

Also known as Dijon Goose, this recipe calls for goose- and chicken-liver stuffing to plump up the bird.

Servings 8 to 10

Total Time ⏳⏳⏳

Major Utensils Roasting pan
Trussing equipment (see page 5)
Medium saucepan
Food mill

Ingredients
1 goose (10-12 pounds), excess fat removed
White wine
Salt and pepper
Nutmeg
Goose liver
½ pound chicken livers
1 cup white wine or Chicken Stock (see page 10)
3 green onions, chopped
1 tablespoon parsley
1 teaspoon chervil
1 teaspoon chives
1 teaspoon basil
1 bay leaf
1 clove of garlic, minced
2 tablespoons butter, melted
2 egg yolks
2½ cups fresh bread crumbs
1 cup orange juice
2 tablespoons currant jelly
Rind of 1 orange, grated
Beurre Manié (see page 56)

Step by Step

1. Brush **goose** inside and out with **white wine,** and dust with **salt, pepper,** and a little **nutmeg.** Set aside.

2. Place **goose liver** and **chicken livers** in a saucepan with **white wine** or **Chicken Stock, green onions, parsley, chervil, chives, bay leaf, basil,** and **garlic.** Bring to boil, and simmer for about 30 minutes, stirring occasionally.

3. Drain livers, reserving the liquid, then put through a food mill. Add **butter, egg yolks,** and **bread crumbs;** mix thoroughly.

4. Stuff goose, truss, and place in roasting pan. Roast at 375°F, calculating 20–25 minutes per pound. Mix liver liquid with **orange juice,** and baste goose frequently. When bird is done, place on a serving platter. Strain and degrease pan juices.

5. Heat pan juices and remaining basting sauce with **currant jelly** and **orange rind** in a saucepan. Thicken slightly with **Beurre Manié.** Pour over the roasted goose.

Goose with Gooseberries

Gooseberries and oranges provide the tangy taste that goose calls for. Gooseberry syrup burnishes the roast to a rich, golden brown.

Servings	8 to 10
Total Time	⧖ ⧖ ⧖
Major Utensils	Roasting pan with rack Trussing equipment (see page 5) Medium saucepan
Ingredients	**1 goose (8 pounds)** **Salt and pepper** **2 large onions** **1 clove of garlic, crushed** **2 teaspoons thyme** **2 cups dry vermouth** **2 large cans gooseberries with syrup** **2 cups mandarin orange sections**
Step by Step	**1.** Sprinkle **goose** cavity with **salt** and **pepper**, and place **onions, garlic**, and **thyme** inside cavity. **2.** Truss bird and place breast down on a rack in a roasting pan. Prick skin to release fat. Baste with **vermouth**, and place in a 325°F oven for 30 minutes. Pour off fat, turn bird onto side, prick skin, and roast, basting occasionally, for another 30 minutes. Repeat procedure for other side. When vermouth is used up, baste with pan juices. **3.** Drain syrup from **gooseberries**. Reserve. **4.** Turn goose breast side up, prick skin, and pour off 2 cups of pan juices; degrease and set aside. Baste bird with gooseberry syrup occasionally while roasting for final 30 minutes, or until goose is tender and well glazed. **5.** Combine gooseberries and **orange sections** in a medium saucepan. Add reserved pan juices and heat through. **6.** Transfer goose to platter, after emptying its cavity of seasoning mixture. Spoon gooseberry-orange mixture and pan juices over it before serving.

Guinea Hen Arlésienne

Arlésienne *refers to the Arles region of France where dishes are often served with sautéed eggplants, (*aubergines meunières*), broiled or fried tomatoes, and fried onion rings.*

Servings	4
Total Time	⧖ ⧖
Major Utensil	Ovenproof skillet with cover
Ingredients	2 guinea hens, skinned and halved ¼ cup butter ¼ cup vegetable oil Salt and pepper 1 cup dry white wine
Side Dishes	Sautéed Eggplant (below) Broiled Tomatoes (see page 81) Fried Onion Rings (see page 73)
Garnish	Croutons (see page 127)
Step by Step	**1.** In a skillet, sauté **guinea hen** pieces in **butter and oil** over medium heat until browned. Season with **salt** and **pepper**. Add **white wine**, cover, and bake at 350°F until tender (about 1 hour). **2.** On a serving platter, surround guinea hen pieces with **Sautéed Eggplant, Broiled Tomatoes,** and **Fried Onion Rings**. Garnish with **Croutons.**

🥘🥘🥘 Sautéed Eggplant

Peel **2 medium eggplants** and cut lengthwise into thin slices. Sprinkle with **salt,** and let stand for 15 minutes. Wipe dry and cut into cubes. Dredge cubes in **flour,** then sauté in ¼ **cup butter** and ¼ **cup oil** in a skillet over medium heat until tender. Combine **3 tablespoons lemon juice** and ½ **cup** very hot **melted butter**; spoon over eggplant. Sprinkle with **chopped parsley.**

Guinea Hen with Coconut Milk

Guinea hen, also known as guinea fowl, has a delicate taste similar to that of pheasant. Indeed, on banquet menus it is sometimes called "Bohemian pheasant."

Servings 2 to 4

Total Time ⏳ ⏳

Major Utensils Large skillet
Casserole with cover

Ingredients **2 guinea hens, cut in pieces (see page 4)**
Salt and pepper
½ cup butter
1 tablespoon lemon juice
½ pound mushrooms, sliced
¾ cup boiling water
¼ cup Coconut Milk (below)
Nutmeg
1 tablespoon cornstarch
1 cup light cream

Step by Step 1. Season **guinea hen** with **salt** and **pepper**. In a skillet over medium heat, sauté lightly in **butter** and **lemon juice**. Arrange meat in a greased casserole, pieces overlapping slightly. Set aside.
2. Add **mushrooms** to skillet, and sauté lightly, adding more butter if needed.
3. Add **boiling water, Coconut Milk,** salt, pepper, and **a pinch of nutmeg** to the skillet; stir thoroughly. Pour over guinea hen. Cover, and bake at 375°F until meat is just tender (about 45 minutes).
4. Blend **cornstarch** and **cream**, and stir into casserole. Return to oven, and bake a further 15 minutes.

🍲🍲🍲 Coconut Milk

Pour **1 cup scalded milk** over **½ pound shredded coconut meat**. Let stand for about 1 hour. Press into wire strainer or squeeze in cheesecloth to extract liquid.

Guinea Hen with Cognac

Cognac added to the guinea hen cavity imparts flavor that penetrates the bird's flesh. More cognac is added to the serving sauce.

Servings	4 to 6
Total Time	⏳ ⏳
Major Utensils	Roasting pan Trussing equipment (see page 5)
Ingredients	**4 guinea hens** **4 green onions, chopped** **4 bay leaves** **Salt and pepper** **Thyme** **½ cup cognac** **Vegetable oil**
Sauce	**Chicken Stock (see page 10)** **¼ cup cognac** **1 cup Brown Sauce (see page 11)** **2 slices of ham, cut in thin strips**
Step by Step	**1.** Inside each **guinea hen** put 1 chopped **green onion, 1 bay leaf,** a pinch of **thyme, salt, pepper,** and **2 tablespoons cognac.** Truss hens (see page 5), and brush with **vegetable oil.** **2.** Place in roasting pan, and bake at 375°F until tender (about 1 hour 30 minutes), basting frequently. Transfer hens to serving platter, and keep hot. **3.** Degrease pan juices; add **Chicken Stock** and blend thoroughly. Add **cognac, Brown Sauce,** and **ham.** Heat and pour over guinea hens.

Use small guinea hens—sometimes called squab—in this recipe. If unavailable, use very small chickens instead.

Guinea Hen with Litchi Nuts

Litchis (or lychees) are stone fruits of Chinese origin. The size of large cherries, litchis have white, firm, and juicy pulp. The fruit is available canned at specialty grocery stores, and is sometimes sold fresh at Oriental markets.

Servings 4

Total Time ⏳ ⏳

Major Utensils Large skillet
Casserole
Small saucepan

Ingredients
2 guinea hens, skinned and cut in pieces (see page 4)
¼ cup butter
¼ cup vegetable oil
½ cup sherry
1 cup Brown Sauce (see page 11)
Juice of 1 orange (⅓ cup)
Coriander
Ginger
Cloves, ground
1 can litchi nuts with syrup

Step by Step
1. In the skillet over medium heat, sauté **guinea hens** in **butter** and **oil** until lightly browned.
2. Place in a greased casserole, and bake at 400°F until hen is tender (about 1 hour). Arrange on serving platter, and keep hot.
3. Add **sherry** to pan juices, and stir thoroughly. Add **Brown Sauce, orange juice,** and **a pinch each of coriander, ginger,** and **cloves.** Cook over medium heat for 5 minutes.
4. In a saucepan, heat **litchi nuts** in **syrup.** Drain, and add fruit to sauce with a few spoonfuls of syrup. Adjust seasoning. Pour over guinea hens.

Braised Turkey Roll

The boneless turkey roll, whether of white and dark meat or white meat only, makes an excellent party roast because it is easy to carve and serve. Turkey rolls are generally available frozen.

Servings 10 to 12

Total Time ⏳ ⏳ ⏳

Major Utensil Roasting pan with cover

Ingredients
1 turkey roll (5 pounds)
2 tablespoons peanut oil
2 tablespoons butter
1½ cups canned mushroom pieces and liquid
3 leeks, sliced
1 teaspoon savory
4 juniper berries, bruised in a mortar
Salt and pepper
3 cups dry red wine
Cornstarch Thickening (below)

Step by Step

1. Dry defrosted **turkey roll**, then brown in the **butter** and **oil** until golden.
2. Drain **mushroom pieces**, reserving **liquid**. Put mushroom, **leeks**, **savory**, and **juniper berries** in roasting pan with turkey roll. Sprinkle with **salt** and **pepper**. Pour ½ **cup of wine** over turkey.
3. Cover, and cook in 350°F oven. Add **remaining wine**, ½ cup at a time, at 20-minute intervals. Add reserved mushroom liquid last. The turkey should be cooked within 2 hours.
4. Slice one side of roll so it will rest flat on serving platter. Place on platter and keep warm.
5. To make gravy, strain or purée pan juices, then add **Cornstarch Thickening**.

Cornstarch Thickening

To thicken 1 cup of liquid, combine **1 tablespoon cornstarch** and **3 tablespoons cold water**; mix into a smooth paste. Blend a little of the hot liquid into the mixture, then add this paste to the sauce.

Lemony Turkey Kabobs

A hint of lemon gives a delightful lift to turkey en brochette. This dish goes well with rice.

Servings 4

Total Time ⏳⏳⏳

Major Utensils Large glass bowl
8 skewers
Broiling pan

Ingredients 1½ pounds turkey breast, boned, skinned, cut in 1-inch cubes (see pages 4 and 5)
1 tablespoon lemon rind, grated
⅓ cup lemon juice
¼ cup vegetable oil
1 tablespoon corn syrup
1 tablespoon cider vinegar
1 clove of garlic, minced
3 small zucchini, cut in 1-inch pieces
½ pound medium mushrooms

Step by Step **1.** In a glass bowl, combine **lemon rind, juice, oil, corn syrup, vinegar,** and **garlic**. Add **turkey cubes**. Cover and refrigerate for at least 2 hours (or overnight). Stir occasionally.
2. Drain turkey, reserving marinade. Thread turkey cubes alternately with **zucchini** and **mushrooms** on 8 skewers.
3. Place skewers on rack of broiler pan. Brush with marinade. Broil approximately 5 inches from burner until turkey is tender (20–25 minutes), rotating skewers and brushing with marinade every 5 minutes.

 To get the most out of a lemon, wash it and chill it thoroughly before grating. Before juicing, bring the lemon to room temperature and roll it between your hands or on a table.

Smoked Turkey in Aspic

This is an elegant and delicious buffet dish to showcase an artistic, gustatorial flair. Most of the preparation time required is for chilling the aspic.

Servings	4 to 6
Total Time	⏳ ⏳ ⏳
Major Utensils	Aspic mold Medium saucepan
Ingredients	**Smoked turkey, skin and fat removed, thinly sliced** 2 cups **Clarified Jellied Consommé** (see page 10) ¼ cup **Madeira** or **sherry** **Hard-cooked eggs, sliced** **Truffles** or **black olives, sliced**
Garnish	1 cup **Clarified Jellied Consommé, diced fine or crushed with a fork** **Sweet pickles, thinly sliced** **Black olives, thinly sliced** **Cherry tomatoes, thinly sliced**
Step by Step	**1.** Melt **Clarified Jellied Consommé** in a saucepan by heating gently. Line oiled aspic mold with a thin layer of consommé, and chill until set. **2.** Decorate with slices of **hard-cooked eggs** and **truffles** or **black olives.** Add another thin layer of consommé to fix decorations; chill until set. Chill remaining consommé until partly set. **3.** Fill mold with alternating layers of **smoked turkey** and partly-set consommé. Chill until set. **4.** Slice **pickles** thin, leaving slices attached at one end; spread into fan shape. Turn aspic out of mold, and garnish with **diced** or **crushed Clarified Jellied Consommé, black olives,** pickle fans, and **cherry tomatoes.**

Peking Duck (see page 114). ▶

Spaghetti with Turkey Sauce

Dark turkey meat is richly flavored; it can hold its own in this spicy tomato sauce.

Servings   4 to 6

Total Time   ⏳ ⏳

Major Utensils   Deep skillet
Large saucepan

Ingredients
1 pound dark turkey meat, diced or ground
¼ cup vegetable oil
Salt and pepper
2 onions, chopped
2 green peppers, chopped
1 teaspoon paprika
½ teaspoon thyme
½ teaspoon chili pepper
1 large can tomatoes
1 small can tomato paste
1 pound spaghetti

Step by Step
1. In a skillet over medium heat, sauté **turkey** meat in **oil**.
2. Add **salt, pepper, onions, green peppers, paprika, thyme, chili pepper, tomatoes,** and **tomato paste**. Simmer for 1 hour.
3. About 10 minutes before serving, cook **spaghetti** in boiling, salted water until tender. Drain, rinse with boiling water, and drain again. Serve with turkey sauce.

Croutons

Dice **fresh** or **dry bread** into ½-inch cubes. Sauté in **butter** until evenly browned. Alternatively, butter slices of bread on both sides before dicing; brown in a moderately hot oven (375°F).

Spicy Turkey Meat Loaf

Equal parts turkey and ground beef blend tastefully in this zesty loaf. A tossed green salad and boiled new potatoes round out a well-balanced meal.

Servings	4 to 6
Total Time	⏳ ⏳
Major Utensils	Medium skillet Loaf pan
Ingredients	**2 cups raw turkey, ground** **2 cups lean ground beef** **3 medium onions, chopped** **½ cup butter** **1 cup Catsup (below)** **2 teaspoons salt**
Step by Step	**1.** In a skillet, sauté the **onions** lightly in **butter** over medium heat. **2.** Grease a loaf pan and spread the onions evenly in it; cover with **Catsup.** **3.** Mix thoroughly the **turkey, beef,** and **salt.** Add to the loaf pan. Bake at 350°F for about 1 hour 30 minutes.

 **Catsup**

Combine ½ **cup tomato sauce, 2 tablespoons sugar, 1 tablespoon vinegar,** and ⅛ **teaspoon ground cloves.** Store tightly covered in refrigerator until needed.

Spinach and Turkey Pie

This dish is an excellent way for using up turkey leftovers. The cooked meat is first soaked in brandy, a procedure that can be done the day before cooking.

Servings   4 to 6

Total Time   ⏳ ⏳ ⏳

Major Utensils   Glass or enamel bowl
Large skillet
Deep pie dish

Ingredients   **1 pound cooked turkey, coarsely chopped**
¼ cup brandy
4 poultry livers, coarsely chopped
6 tablespoons butter
½ pound mushrooms, coarsely chopped
2 eggs, beaten
2 green onions, chopped
½ teaspoon thyme
1½ teaspoons parsley
Salt and pepper
Pie Pastry for two crusts (see page 75)
4 slices ham, cut in strips
1 pound raw spinach

Step by Step   **1.** In a glass or enamel bowl, soak the **turkey** in **brandy** for 6 hours.
2. In a skillet over high heat, sear **poultry livers** in **butter**. Remove from pan, reduce heat to medium, and sauté **mushrooms** lightly in remaining butter. Add turkey, livers, **eggs, green onions, thyme, parsley, and salt** and **pepper, to taste**.
3. Roll out **Pie Pastry,** and line pie dish. Distribute strips of **ham** evenly on the bottom. Cover with meat mixture, then with **spinach**. Cover with pastry, sealing well around the edges. Cut vents.
4. Bake at 375°F until crust is deep golden.

Marinate the turkey in a glazed ceramic or glass bowl that is just large enough to contain the meat. Whenever meat is to be marinated for longer than 1 hour, it should be placed in the refrigerator.

Turkey Balls

Leftover turkey can be easily stored when rolled into balls and placed in the freezer. Cooked turkey balls are versatile: they go well with potatoes or rice, and with a variety of creamy sauces.

Servings	4
Total Time	⏳
Major Utensil	Medium, deep skillet
Ingredients	½ pound cooked turkey, minced
	4 slices of white bread, crust removed
	1 egg, beaten
	1½ tablespoons lemon juice (½ lemon, juiced)
	Salt and pepper
	½ cup vegetable oil

Step by Step

1. Soak **bread** slices in water until wet. Squeeze dry.
2. Blend **turkey,** bread, and **egg.** Season to taste with **salt** and **pepper.**
3. Roll into small balls (or wrap carefully and freeze).
4. In the skillet over medium–high heat, brown turkey balls in hot **oil** until golden.

To vary this recipe, add one or more of the following ingredients: 1 small minced onion, lightly sautéed in butter; 1 small minced clove of garlic, lightly sautéed in butter; 1 tablespoon parsley flakes; a pinch of thyme or sage.

Turkey Chop Suey

Chop sueys are combinations of meat and bean sprouts served over rice. If using canned bean sprouts, add them at the last minute, and heat through before serving.

Servings	4 to 6
Total Time	⌛
Major Utensil	Large, deep skillet
Ingredients	**2 cups raw turkey** **Salt and pepper** **¼ cup vegetable oil** **2 tablespoons flour** **2 onions, chopped** **2 stalks of celery, diced** **2 cups Chicken Stock (see page 10)** **2 tablespoons soy sauce** **1 pound fresh bean sprouts**
Side Dish	**Boiled Rice (see page 70)**
Step by Step	**1.** Season **turkey** with **salt** and **pepper,** and, in a large skillet over medium heat, sauté lightly in hot **oil.** **2.** Add **flour,** and cook for 2–3 minutes, stirring. Add **onions** and **celery,** and continue to stir-fry until crisp, yet tender. **3.** Meanwhile, combine **Chicken Stock** and **soy sauce.** Pour into turkey and vegetables. Simmer for about 30 minutes. **4.** While turkey cooks, prepare **Boiled Rice.** **5.** Stir **bean sprouts** into turkey mixture and simmer for 10 minutes. Serve with rice.

Turkey-Cranberry Aspic

To display this aspic's colorful layers, slice it and serve the individual portions on a bed of bright-green lettuce leaves.

Servings	6
Total Time	⏳ ⏳ ⏳
Major Utensils	Double boiler Loaf pan Medium saucepan

Ingredients Layer 1

2 tablespoons gelatin
¼ cup cold water
1 medium can cranberry sauce
1 cup crushed pineapple (with juice)
Juice of 1 lemon (3 tablespoons)

Step by Step

1. Soften **gelatin** in cold **water** in double-boiler top. Dissolve it over boiling water.
2. Add **cranberry sauce, pineapple,** and **lemon juice,** and mix well. Pour into an oiled loaf pan and chill until firm (about 2 hours).

Ingredients Layer 2

4 cups cooked turkey, chopped
2 tablespoons gelatin
¼ cup cold water
1 cup Turkey Stock (see page 10)
½ cup Mayonnaise (see page 42)
1 cup celery, chopped

Step by Step

1. Soften **gelatin** in cold **water.** In a saucepan, bring the **Turkey Stock** to boil; add gelatin and stir until dissolved.
2. When cool, add **Mayonnaise, celery,** and **turkey.** Pour over first mixture and refrigerate overnight. Unmold before serving.

Turkey Hash

Here's what might be called a "throw-together" meal. It's easy, it's filling, it's a great way to use up leftovers. To experiment, add whatever vegetables are on hand.

Servings 4

Total Time ⏳

Major Utensil Large skillet

Ingredients
1 cup cooked turkey, finely chopped
½ cup celery, sliced
2 tablespoons onion, minced
2 tablespoons butter
2 cups (3 medium) cooked potatoes, diced
⅔ cup milk
Salt and pepper
Paprika

Step by Step
1. In the skillet over medium heat, sauté **celery** and **onion** in **butter** until tender.
2. Add **turkey, potatoes,** and **milk.** Cook slowly, stirring occasionally until heated through. Add **salt, pepper,** and **paprika,** to taste.
3. Increase heat to brown the hash.

🫕🫕🫕 Turkey Scallops

Skin an uncooked, partially frozen **turkey breast**. Or remove skin from the breast of a partially frozen whole turkey. Place breast flat on a cutting board and slice thinly across the surface. One medium breast should yield 5 scallops. If cutting scallops from whole turkey, first cut slantwise behind the wishbone to get an additional scallop. It is not necessary to remove the whole breast before slicing scallops.

Turkey Potpie

This uncomplicated recipe uses condensed mushroom soup as the sauce base; the pie crust is made from cheese.

Servings 4

Total Time ⌛

Major Utensil Flameproof casserole

Ingredients
2 cups cooked or raw turkey, diced
¼ cup vegetable shortening
1 can cream of mushroom soup
1 cup milk
1 cup green peas
1 green pepper, diced
Salt and pepper
Cheese Pastry (see page 45)

Step by Step
1. In a casserole over medium heat, sauté diced, cooked **turkey** lightly in vegetable shortening. (If raw turkey is used, sauté it over low heat for 20 minutes.)
2. Combine **mushroom soup** and **milk**. Season with **salt** and **pepper**, add **peas** and **green pepper**, and stir into turkey. Cover with **Cheese Pastry**.
3. Bake at 425°F until pastry is golden, about 30 minutes.

♥♥♥ Poultry Seasoning

In a small jar, combine **1 tablespoon thyme, 1 tablespoon marjoram, 1 tablespoon savory,** and **½ tablespoon sage.** Shake jar to blend seasonings. Cover tightly with lid until needed.

Turkey Scallops Cordon-Bleu

The French expression cordon-bleu *literally means* blue ribbon. *In culinary terms, it refers to dishes with ham and cheese as ingredients.*

Servings	4
Total Time	⏳
Major Utensil	Large skillet
Ingredients	**4 Turkey Scallops (see page 133)** **Seasoned Flour (see page 28)** **4 slices of lean boiled ham** **6 tablespoons butter** **4-6 ounces mushrooms, sliced** **4 thin slices of fontina, Bel Paese, or Gruyère cheese** **1 tablespoon olive oil** **Pepper** **1-2 tablespoons parsley** **4-6 tablespoons Chicken Stock, hot (see page 10)**
Garnish	**Watercress**
Step by Step	**1.** Coat **Turkey Scallops** evenly, but not too thickly, with **Seasoned Flour.** **2.** Cook the **mushrooms** until soft in **1 tablespoon of the butter**, and set them aside. **3.** Meanwhile, trim the **ham** and **cheese slices** to fit the scallops. **4.** Melt the **remaining butter** and the **oil** in the large skillet over medium heat. Sauté the scallops for about 5 minutes on each side. **5.** Place a slice of ham on each scallop, spoon over a thin layer of mushrooms, and season lightly with freshly ground **pepper.** Sprinkle a little of the **parsley** over the mushrooms and cover with a slice of cheese. **6.** Pour the hot **Chicken Stock** over the scallops. Cover the pan closely with a lid of foil and cook over low heat for about 10 minutes or until the cheese has melted. **7.** Lift out the scallops and arrange on a hot serving dish; sprinkle with the **remaining parsley** or garnish with sprigs of **watercress.**

This recipe is illustrated on page 143.

Turkey Scallops Mirabel

Turkey scallops are thin slices of turkey breast. Most butchers will prepare them on request, though cooks can slice them easily from a partially frozen bird. One half breast yields about 5 scallops.

Servings   12

Total Time   ⧖ ⧖

Major Utensils   Large skillet
Casserole with cover

Ingredients
12 Turkey Scallops (see page 133)
1 slice of bread, ground into crumbs
1 egg, lightly beaten
1 small onion, finely chopped and lightly sautéed
½ pound ground turkey
½ pound ground pork
½ cup grated Cheddar or Gruyère cheese
½ cup parsley, chopped
2 cloves of garlic, crushed
Salt and pepper
½ cup butter
½ cup oil

Mirabel Sauce
1 cup Brown Sauce (see page 11)
1 cup Tomato Sauce (see page 11)
1 cup white wine

Garnish   ½ cup parsley, chopped

Step by Step

1. Stir together **bread crumbs** and **egg**. Add **onion, turkey, pork, cheese, parsley, garlic, salt,** and **pepper**.

2. Spread this stuffing on **Turkey Scallops**. Roll and truss with string. In a skillet over medium heat, sauté rolled fillets in **butter** and **oil** until light brown. Cool.

3. Meanwhile, prepare **Mirabel Sauce** by blending **Brown Sauce, Tomato Sauce,** and **white wine**.

4. Remove string from cooled scallops and arrange in a casserole. Pour sauce over scallops. Cover, and bake at 350°F for 1 hour.

5. Arrange rolled turkey scallops on a serving platter, and keep hot. Skim excess fat from sauce and boil over high heat to reduce by half. Pour over turkey, and sprinkle with **parsley**.

Turkey Soufflé with Olives

This soufflé takes only about 15 minutes to prepare. The olives and turkey provide complementary flavors and textures.

Servings	4
Total Time	⏳ ⏳
Major Utensil	Soufflé dish
Ingredients	2 cups cooked turkey, minced ¼ cup Garlic Butter (below) 4 slices of bread 4 eggs, separated 2 cups milk Salt and pepper ½ cup green, stuffed olives, sliced
Step by Step	1. Spread **Garlic Butter** on **bread**, and cut into small cubes. 2. Beat **egg yolks**, and add **milk, salt, pepper, olives**, and bread cubes; stir into minced **turkey**. 3. Beat **egg whites** until stiff; fold gently into the first mixture. 4. Spoon into a greased soufflé dish (it should be three-quarters full). Bake at 325°F for 1 hour. Serve immediately.

Garlic Butter

Combine **4 cloves of crushed garlic** with **½ cup soft butter**. If time allows, let stand for 30 minutes so garlic permeates butter.

Turkey Stuffed with Potatoes

Potato stuffing captures the turkey juices while it helps to keep the bird moist. It can be prepared a day ahead. This recipe includes a butter-mustard paste that eliminates basting.

Servings   10 to 12

Total Time   ⏳ ⏳ ⏳

Major Utensils   Roasting pan
Trussing equipment (see page 5)
Medium saucepan

Ingredients
1 turkey (12 pounds)
Potato Stuffing (see page 139)
1 thick, dry crust of bread
¼ small onion
9 tablespoons butter
1 whole nutmeg
½ lemon
2 tablespoons dry mustard
1 tablespoon salt
½ teaspoon pepper
3 tablespoons flour
Salt pork, thinly sliced

Gravy
2 cups pan juices and/or Poultry Stock (see page 10)
2 cups cold tea
½ cup turkey fat
½ cup flour
1 cup red wine
Salt and pepper

Step by Step

1. Stuff **turkey** with **Potato Stuffing**. (See pages 5 and 6 for instructions on stuffing and trussing poultry.)

2. Rub **dry bread crust** with **onion**; spread on **1 tablespoon butter**. Place inside opening over stuffing. Truss the turkey.

3. Place turkey in the roasting pan. Rub the skin with **nutmeg**, grating nutmeg occasionally to draw out the oil. Rub skin with **lemon**.

4. Cream together **remaining butter, mustard, salt, pepper,** and **flour**. Rub this paste over the turkey breast and legs.

5. Wrap the legs with **salt pork slices**.

6. Place in a 325°F oven and cook until bird is tender (about 4 hours). Do not baste; avoid opening the oven.

7. Transfer turkey to a warm platter and keep warm while preparing gravy.

8. Skim fat from **pan juices**. If remaining juice measures less than two cups, add enough **Poultry Stock** to make up the difference.

Step by Step Continued

9. Meanwhile, put the roasting pan over medium heat and add the **tea.** Bring to boil, stirring constantly and scraping pan bottom.
10. Blend **fat** and **flour** in a saucepan and cook gently until medium brown.
11. Stir in the tea-pan juice mixture and the **wine.** Cook over medium heat until thickened. Season to taste with **salt** and **pepper.** Strain, and serve with turkey.

Potato Stuffing

Grind or mince **turkey giblets.** Melt **4 tablespoons butter** in a medium skillet and add **3 large minced onions** and **1 minced clove of garlic.** Cook over low heat until onions are soft. Add giblets, and stir over high heat until brown. Mash **10 cups hot, cooked potatoes** in a large bowl. Add the browned onions, garlic, and giblets. Season with approximately **1 tablespoon salt,** ½ **teaspoon pepper,** 1½ **teaspoons savory,** and ½ **teaspoon dry mustard.** Blend in **3 tablespoons melted butter.**

Potatoes that have been stored in the vegetable compartment of a refrigerator develop a sugary flavor that many people find distasteful. To eliminate this flavor, put the potatoes in warm storage (above 70°F) for several weeks. During this period, the sugars will convert back to starch, and the spud will once more taste as it should.

Turkey with Broccoli

Broccoli stems, as well as florets, add texture in addition to flavor to this stir-fry dish. Serve with rice.

Servings 4

Total Time ⏳

Major Utensil Wok

Ingredients
1 small turkey breast (1 pound), cut in thin strips
½ cup water
1 tablespoon cornstarch
2 tablespoons soy sauce
¼ teaspoon ginger
6 tablespoons vegetable oil
½ pound mushrooms, sliced
1 head of broccoli (½ pound); stems cut in ¼-inch slices, florets in bite-size pieces
1 teaspoon salt

Step by Step
1. In a small bowl, combine ¼ **cup of water, cornstarch, soy sauce,** and **ginger.** Set aside.
2. In a wok, heat **4 tablespoons of oil.** Add **turkey** and stir-fry 1 minute.
3. Add **mushrooms;** stir-fry 30 seconds. Remove turkey and mushrooms from wok; set aside.
4. Add remaining **2 tablespoons of oil, broccoli stems,** and **salt.** Stir-fry 30 seconds.
5. Add **broccoli florets** and stir-fry 1 minute. Add remaining ¼ **cup of water;** cover and cook over medium heat 3 minutes.
6. Return turkey and mushrooms to wok; stir-fry on *High* 1 minute.
7. Push turkey and vegetables up side of wok; stir cornstarch mixture, gradually, into boiling liquid. Cook until thick and clear, stirring constantly. Mix meat and vegetables into sauce.

Ingredient Substitutions

Ingredient	Amount	Substitute
Bread crumbs, fine, dry	1 cup	¾ cup cracker crumbs or 4 slices of stale bread, crumbed
Bread crumbs, soft	1 cup	2 slices of fresh bread, crumbed
Butter	1 cup	¾ cup clarified poultry fat or ⅞ cup shortening plus ½ teaspoon salt
Chicken broth	1 cup	1 bouillon cube dissolved in 1 cup boiling water
Cornstarch as thickener	1 tablespoon	2 tablespoons flour
Cream, heavy	1 cup	¾ cup milk plus ⅓ cup melted butter
Cream, light	1 cup	¾ cup milk plus ¼ cup melted butter
Garlic	1 small clove	⅛ teaspoon garlic powder
Ginger, powdered	¼ teaspoon	2 tablespoons minced ginger root
Herbs, fresh	1 tablespoon	1 teaspoon dried herbs or ⅔ teaspoon ground herbs
Lemon juice	1 teaspoon	½ teaspoon vinegar
Lemon rind, grated	1 teaspoon	½ teaspoon lemon extract
Mushrooms, fresh	8 ounces	1 6-ounce can mushrooms, drained
Mustard, prepared	1 tablespoon	1 teaspoon dry mustard
Onion	1 small	1 tablespoon dry, minced onion or 1 teaspoon onion powder
Sour cream	1 cup	⅞ cup yogurt or buttermilk plus 3 tablespoons butter
Tomatoes, chopped	1⅓ cups	1 cup canned tomatoes
Tomato paste	1 tablespoon	1 tablespoon catsup
Tomato sauce	2 cups	¾ cup tomato paste plus 1 cup water

Recipes by Name and Time

Fast recipes, taking less than 1 hour to prepare and cook, are highlighted in **bold** type.

CHICKEN
Asparagus-Chicken Casserole, 12
Avocado-Chicken Casserole, 13
Barbecued Chicken, 14
Boer Chicken Pie, 15
Chicken and Pork Pie, 16
Chicken Antonia, 19
Chicken Ballottine, 20–21
Chicken Breasts in Sherry, 22
Chicken Breasts Milano, 23
Chicken Brochettes, 24
Chicken Cacciatore, 25
Chicken Chaud-Froid, 26–27
Chicken Cordon-Bleu, 28
Chicken Croquettes, 29
Chicken Flambé with Cream, 30
Chicken Fricassee, 31
Chicken Hot Pot, 32
Chicken in Red Wine, 33
Chicken Jambalaya, 34
Chicken Kiev, 37
Chicken Lasagna, 38
Chicken Leg Ring, 39
Chicken Legs Chaud-Froid, 40–41
Chicken Log, 42
Chicken Madrid, 43
Chicken Maryland, 44
Chicken Pie with Cheese Pastry, 45
Chicken Poached with Potatoes, 46
Chicken Provence Style, 47
Chicken Saint Sylvester, 48
Chicken Salad, 49
Chicken Sauté with Madeira, 50
Chicken Stew with Okra, 51
Chicken Tetrazzini, 52
Chicken Torcello, 55
Chicken Vienna, 56
Chicken Wings with Mushrooms, 57
Chicken with Garlic, 58
Chicken with Mushrooms, 59
Chicken with Orange and Onion, 60
Chicken with Rice Pilaf, 61
Chicken with Sautéed Vegetables, 62
Chicken with Sour Cream, 63
Chicken with Truffles, 64
Chinese Chicken Casserole, 65
Chinese Deviled Chicken, 66
Coq au Vin, 67
Crêpes à la King, 68
Crunchy Almond Chicken, 69
Curried Chicken, 70
Curried Chicken Salad, 73
Deep-Fried Chicken, 74
Deviled Chicken, 75
French Roasted Chicken, 76
Gardener's Chicken, 77
Golden Baked Chicken, 78
Golden Glazed Broilers, 79
Hungarian Chicken, 80
Lemon-Chicken Catalan, 81
Miniature Chicken Balls, 82
Mushroom-Chicken and Artichokes, 83
Orange-Glazed Chicken, 84
Oriental Chicken, 85
Oven-Poached Creamy Chicken, 86
Oyster-Chicken Casserole, 87
Paella, 88
Pineapple-Chicken Casserole, 91
Quick Chicken Casserole, 92
Roquefort Chicken, 93
Spiced Chicken and Rice, 94–95
Sugar-Broiled Chicken, 96
Tarragon Chicken, 97
Teriyaki Chicken, 98
Zucchini-Chicken with Orange, 99

CHICKEN LIVERS
Chicken Liver Pâté, 100
Chicken Livers with Grapes, 101
Sweet and Sour Chicken Livers, 102

CORNISH HEN
Cornish Hen with Sausage, 103

DUCK
Duck Breasts in Pastry, 104
Duck in Orange Sauce, 105
Duck in Wine Sauce, 106
Duck in the Apple Orchard, 109
Duck with Green Peas, 110
Duck with Peaches, 111
Duck with Turnip, 112
Duck with Vegetables, 113
Peking Duck, 114–115

GOOSE
Goose in Orange Sauce, 116
Goose with Gooseberries, 117

GUINEA HEN
Guinea Hen Arlésienne, 118
Guinea Hen with Coconut Milk, 119
Guinea Hen with Cognac, 120
Guinea Hen with Litchi Nuts, 121

TURKEY
Braised Turkey Roll, 122
Lemony Turkey Kabobs, 123
Smoked Turkey in Aspic, 124
Spaghetti with Turkey Sauce, 127
Spicy Turkey Meat Loaf, 128
Spinach and Turkey Pie, 129
Turkey Balls, 130
Turkey Chop Suey, 131
Turkey-Cranberry Aspic, 132
Turkey Hash, 133
Turkey Potpie, 134
Turkey Scallops Cordon-Bleu, 135
Turkey Scallops Mirabel, 136
Turkey Soufflé with Olives, 137
Turkey Stuffed with Potatoes, 138–139
Turkey with Broccoli, 140

Turkey Scallops Cordon-Bleu (see page 135).▲
Chicken Livers with Grapes (see page 101).▶

chicken jambalaya, 34
paella, 88
prepared shrimp, 34
spiced chicken with rice, 94
Seasoned flour, 28
Sesame seeds
   teriyaki chicken, 98
Sherry, chicken breasts in, 22
Shrimp. *See* Seafood
Sour cream, chicken with, 63
Spinach and turkey pie, 129
Stewed tomatoes, 51
Stock
   clarified, 10
   giblet, 105
   light chicken, 31
   poultry (chicken or turkey), 10
   asparagus-chicken casserole, 12
   chicken Antonia, 19
   chicken Madrid, 43
   chicken poached with potatoes, 46
   chicken Torcello, 55
   chicken with rice pilaf, 61
   coq au vin, 67
   curried chicken, 70
   duck with green peas, 110
   goose in orange sauce, 116
   lemon-chicken Catalan, 81
   mushroom-chicken and artichokes, 83
   turkey chop suey, 131
   turkey-cranberry aspic, 132
   veal
      chicken with truffles, 64
Stuffing
   almond dressing, 41
   apple, 8
   bread or cracker, 8
   celery, 8
   celery-apricot, 8
   chestnut, 9
   cranberry, 9
   giblet, 8
   herb, 8
   mushroom, 8
   potato, 139
   rice, 9

   sausage, 9
   veal forcemeat, 9
Sugarless catsup, 66
Supreme sauce, 11
Sweet and sour sauce, 102
Tarragon chicken, 97
Thick gravy, 10
Tomato brown sauce, 11
Tomato sauce, 11
Tomatoes
   broiled, 81
   catsup, 128
   chicken cacciatore, 25
   chicken jambalaya, 34
   chicken lasagna, 38
   chicken Torcello, 55
   spaghetti with turkey sauce, 127
   stewed, 51
   sugarless catsup, 66
   tomato brown sauce, 11
Truffles, chicken with, 64
Turkey scallops, 133
Turkey stock, 10
Turnip, duck with, 112
Veal
   chicken ballottine, 20–21
   chicken legs chaud-froid, 40–41
   chicken with truffles, 64
   duck pâté, 104
   forcemeat stuffing, 9
Vegetables, mixed
   Boer chicken pie, 15
   chicken Antonia, 19
   chicken hot pot, 32
   chicken pie with cheese pastry, 45
   chicken Vienna, 56
   chicken with rice pilaf, 61
   chicken with sautéed, 62
   chicken with truffles, 64
   Chinese chicken casserole, 65
   coq au vin, 67
   duck with, 113
   gardener's chicken, 77
   oriental chicken, 85
   tarragon chicken, 97
   turkey chop suey, 131

Veloutée sauce, 11
Water chestnuts
   Chinese chicken casserole, 65
   oriental chicken, 85
White sauce, 11
Wine. *See also* Brandy and liqueur
   chicken lasagna, 38
   cognac, guinea hen with, 120
   Madeira, chicken sauté with, 50
   red
      braised turkey roll, 122
      chicken in, 33
      chicken Saint Sylvester, 48
      coq au vin, 67
      duck in wine sauce, 106
      duck with vegetables, 113
      turkey stuffed with potatoes, 138–139
   sherry, chicken breasts in, 22
   vermouth
      oyster-chicken casserole, 87
      goose with gooseberries, 117
   white
      avocado-chicken casserole, 13
      chicken cacciatore, 25
      chicken flambé with cream, 30
      chicken Tetrazzini, 52
      duck with turnip or olives, 112
      goose in orange sauce, 116
      guinea hen Arlésienne, 118
      turkey scallops Mirabel, 136
      zucchini-chicken with orange, 99
Yams
   pineapple-chicken casserole, 91
Zucchini
   -chicken with orange, 99
   lemony turkey kabobs, 123

Acknowledgments

Grateful acknowledgment is made for permission to use and adapt recipes from the following sources. Note that when the recipe title differs from the title under which the recipe originally appeared, the original title is given in parentheses.

Canadian Turkey Marketing Agency "Lemony Turkey Kabobs," from *Recipes for the New Turkey;* "Turkey Hash," "Turkey with Broccoli," from *Turkey Anytime.* Reprinted by permission of the Canadian Turkey Marketing Agency.

Editions Mirabel/Invi "Barbecued Chicken" ("Poulets grillés"), "Chicken and Pork Pie" ("Pâté au poulet et au porc"), "Chicken Ballottine" ("Ballottine de poulet"), "Chicken Breasts in Sherry" ("Suprêmes de volaille au sherry"), "Chicken Brochettes" ("Poulet en brochettes"), "Chicken Cacciatore" ("Poulet chasseur"), "Chicken Croquettes" ("Croquettes de poulet"), "Chicken Flambé with Cream" ("Poulet sauté à la crème"), "Chicken Kiev" ("Poulet à la Kiev"), "Chicken Lasagna" ("Lasagne au poulet"), "Chicken Leg Ring" ("Cuisses de poulet en couronne"), "Chicken Legs Chaud-Froid" ("Cuisses de poulet chaud-froid duc de Chartres"), "Chicken Log" ("Rouleau au poulet"), "Chicken Madrid" ("Poulet Madrid"), "Chicken Pie with Cheese Pastry" ("Pâté au poulet avec pâte au fromage"), "Chicken Provence Style" ("Poulet sauté à la provençale"), "Chicken Sauté with Madeira" ("Poulet sauté au madère"), "Chicken Vienna" ("Poulet à la viennoise"), "Chicken Wings with Mushrooms" ("Ailes de poulet aux champignons"), "Chicken with Garlic" ("Poulet à l'ail"), "Chicken with Mushrooms" ("Poulet sauté aux champignons"), "Chicken with Rice Pilaf" ("Poulet au riz—sauce suprême"), "Chicken with Sautéed Vegetables" ("Poulet sauté jardinière"), "Chicken with Truffles" ("Poulet Mère Brazier"), "Coq au vin," "Crêpes à la King" ("Crêpes de poulet à la reine"), "Curried Chicken" ("Poulet au curry"), "Miniature Chicken Balls" ("Petites boulettes au poulet"), "Mushroom-Chicken and Artichokes" ("Poulet sauté aux artichauts"), "Orange-Glazed Chicken" ("Poulet glacé à l'orange et aux amandes"), "Tarragon Chicken" ("Poulet à l'estragon"), "Zucchini-Chicken with Orange" ("Poulet sauté à la grecque"), "Chicken Liver Pâté" ("Pâté de foies de poulet"), "Cornish Hen with Sausage" ("Poussins de casserole—Cornish Hens"), "Duck in Wine Sauce" ("Civet de canard"), "Duck with Green Peas" ("Canard braisé aux petits pois"), "Duck with Peaches" ("Canard aux pêches"), "Duck with Turnip" ("Canard aux navets"), "Goose in Orange Sauce" ("Oie dijonnaise"), "Guinea Hen Arlésienne" ("Pintades à l'arlésienne"), "Guinea Hen with Coconut Milk" ("Pintades au lait de coco"), "Guinea Hen with Cognac" ("Pintades au cognac"), "Guinea Hen with Litchi Nuts" ("Pintades aux lychées"), "Smoked Turkey in Aspic" ("Dinde fumée en aspic"), "Spaghetti with Turkey Sauce" ("Spaghetti avec sauce à la dinde"), "Spicy Turkey Meat Loaf" ("Pain de viande à la sauce piquante"), "Spinach and Turkey Pie" ("Tarte aux épinards et à la viande"), "Turkey Chop Suey" ("Chop Suey à la dinde"), "Turkey-Cranberry Aspic" ("Aspic de dinde aux atocas"), "Turkey Potpie" ("Casserole à la dinde"), "Turkey Scallops Mirabel" ("Paupiettes de dinde Mirabel"), "Turkey Soufflé with Olives" ("Soufflé à la dinde"), from *La cuisine de Monique Chevrier, sa technique, ses recettes.* Copyright © Ottawa, Canada, 1978, Editions Mirabel/Invi. Reprinted by permission of Editions Mirabel/Invi.

The Ontario Chicken Producers' Marketing Board "Oriental Chicken" ("Almond Chicken with Snow Peas"), "Sweet and Sour Chicken Livers," from *Wok Cooking with Chicken;* "Chicken Jambalaya," "Crunchy Almond Chicken," "Roquefort Chicken," from *Chicken in Every Pot;* "Chicken Cordon-Bleu," "Chicken with Sour Cream" ("Bosom de Poulet"), from *Chicken with a Creative Flair.* Reprinted by permission of the Ontario Chicken Producers' Marketing Board.

The Reader's Digest Association (Canada) Ltd., Montreal "Spiced Chicken and Rice," "Teriyaki Chicken," from *Creative Cooking.* Copyright © 1977 The Reader's Digest Association (Canada) Ltd.

The Reader's Digest Association, Inc. "Chicken Antonia," "Chicken Fricassee," "Chicken Poached with Potatoes," "Chicken Salad," "Chicken Stew with Okra," "Chicken Torcello," "Chicken with Oranges and Onion," "Chinese Deviled Chicken," "Deep-Fried Chicken," "Deviled Chicken," "French Roasted Chicken," "Golden Baked Chicken," "Golden Glazed Broilers," "Lemon-Chicken Catalan" ("Chicken Catalan"), "Oven-Poached Creamy Chicken," "Sugar-Broiled Chicken," "Duck in the Apple Orchard," "Duck with Vegetables" ("Roast Duck with Vegetables"), "Goose with Gooseberries," "Braised Turkey Roll," "Turkey Stuffed with Potatoes" ("Roasted Turkey with Potato Stuffing"), from *Secrets of Better Cooking.* Adapted from *My Secrets for Better Cooking* by Jehane Benoît. Copyright © 1973 The Reader's Digest Association, Inc. Reprinted by permission of Jehane Benoît.

The Reader's Digest Association Limited, London, England "Chicken Chaud-Froid," "Chicken in Red Wine," "Chicken Maryland," "Chicken Saint Sylvester" ("Suprêmes de volaille St-Sylvestre"), "Chicken Livers with Grapes," "Gardener's Chicken," "Duck Breasts in Pastry" ("Duck Breasts en Croûte"), "Duck in Orange Sauce" ("Le Caneton à l'Orange"), "Peking Duck," "Turkey Scallops Cordon-Bleu," ("Turkey Escalopes Cordon-Bleu"), from *Cookery Year.* Copyright © 1973. The Reader's Digest Association Limited, London.

Summerhill Press Ltd. "Chicken Tetrazzini," from *Italian Gourmet Cooking.* Copyright © 1980 Pasquale Carpino. Reprinted by permission of Summerhill Press Ltd.

Volunteer Committee of Art Gallery of Windsor "Asparagus Chicken" ("Chicken and Asparagus Casserole"), "Avocado-Chicken Casserole" ("Chicken and Avocado Casserole"), "Boer Chicken Pie," "Chicken Breasts Milano," "Chinese Chicken," "Curried Chicken Salad," "Hungarian Chicken," "Oyster-Chicken Casserole" ("Oyster Mushroom Chicken Casserole"), "Paella," "Pineapple-Chicken Casserole" ("Chicken and Pineapple Casserole"), "Quick Chicken Casserole" ("Speedy Chicken Casserole"), from *The Uncommon Cook Book.* Copyright © 1980 by the Volunteer Committee of the Art Gallery of Windsor. Reprinted by permission of the Volunteer Committee of the Art Gallery of Windsor.